Safe As Houses

Childhood Through the Forties

Margaret Siddall

GW00320001

dh

Devonshire House

1995

In memory of my parents
and dedicated to Kirsty, Emma and Ashley
and grandchildren who may follow.

Cover illustrations a flying bomb;
David, Nigel and Margaret 1940;
St Martin-in-the-Fields High School;
the DVS Magazine; a Morrison shelter

Published in 1995 by Devonshire House
Christow Devon EX6 7LU

British Library Cataloguing in Publication Data.
A catalogue record for this book
is available from the British Library.

ISBN 0 9524513 1 X

Printed and bound in Great Britain by
Abbot Litho Press Ltd

Contents

Illustrations   5

Preview   7

Chapters:

1. Setting Scenes: 1934-1939   9
2. They Wouldn't Bomb Our Little School: Wiltshire 1939-1941   19
3. Down in the Underworld: Swansea 1941-1942   30
4. Flying Over the Trees: 1942-1943   46
5. They're Only Practising: Beckenham 1943   57
6. The House on the Corner: Dulwich 1943-1944   66
7. Flying Bombs and V2s: 1944-1945   85
8. Peace: 1945-1946   98
9. Always Devizes: 1946   121
10. The Black Rovers: 1946-1947   137
11. Beyond the War: 1947-1948   152
12. Almost Grown-Up: 1949-1952   172

Tailpiece: 1995   191

Acknowledgements

Bibliography

Section of Green Family Tree

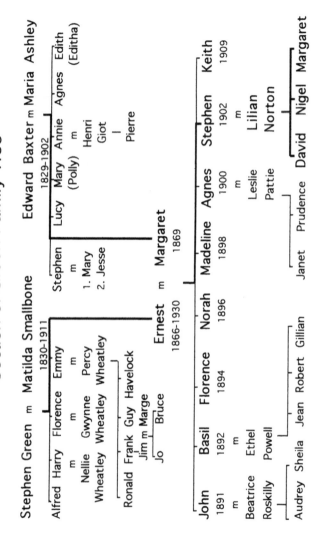

Illustrations

Frontispiece	Green family tree	4
One	They began their married life	
	in Yorkshire	10
	On holiday in the Isle of Wight	10
	Madeline and Florence	14
Two	Life continued as normally	
	as possible	22
	Nigel became a warden too	23
	Picking flowers for our 'shop'	24
Three	The centre of Swansea had been	
	destroyed	33
	My cousin Audrey was a landgirl	38
	The Swiss Cottage Singleton Park	41
	The Educational Gardens	41
Four	The Gower Road, Swansea	49
	I liked Milly-Molly-Mandy	53
Five	We stood by the rockery	59
	Grandpa's house	59
	We climbed inside the hammock	59
Six	We called it the dining room	68
	St Martin-in-the-Fields High School	77
	Nigel made up a junior crossword	82
Seven	A dark cylindrical shape in the sky	85
	Tigger	87
	Careless talk costs lives	90
Eight	Toll House and Toll Gate, Dulwich	109
	Drinking Fountain	109
	The M.G. Enterprises	111
Nine	Map of Devizes	120
	A vast quantity of tiny stationery	124
	Nigel's bedroom above the kitchen	127
Ten	Sledging with Stuart	140
	The thaw started	141
	The Rover contents page	144
	Father camped on his own	150

Eleven   Low tide at West Beach   153
                The old windmill   154
                We stood outside our old house   158
                String stretched across the
                crossroads   164
                Steamers chugged by   169
Twelve   Chestfield Oasthouse   175
                Disciplined, rhythmic gymnastics   184
                School group by the tennis court   184
                The dancing display   184
                The bungalow at Harpsden   190

Abbreviations
AFS—Auxiliary Fire Service
ARP—Air Raid Precautions
ATS—Auxiliary Territorial Service
CCF—Combined Cadet Force
EWS—Emergency Water Supply
LDV—Local Defence Volunteers; later the Home Guard
M & B—May and Baker sulphonamide tablets
MPI—Mean Point of Impact
PNEU—Parents' National Educational Union
V1—Vergeltungswaffe (vengeance weapon)
V2—Vergeltungswaffe supersonic rocket
VE—Victory in Europe
VJ—Victory over Japan
WVS—Women's Voluntary Service; later WRVS
2s 6d—two shillings and sixpence

Preview

David told me I was bought from a china stall in Peckham Market, but older brothers are like that. Why a china stall I had no idea, and I was never sure whether it was really true. Then I reasoned there were no other children for sale in Peckham Market. Even so, the vague possibility lingered with me.

Memories like this have merged into another time scale for me – vivid, nostalgic, individualistic. But when did each one happen? Was our ride on the sledge before we made those coins from the lead markings on the disused tennis courts, or after the flying bomb fell almost opposite? Did we sneak round to sell books to Salkeld, the secondhand bookshop, before or after the imaginary spy threw slates from the church roof?

Fortunately, our various family moves have enabled me to pin-point many incidents in their settings. So the day Nigel – my other brother – and I had secondhand black bicycles, and I learnt to ride, must have been after September 1943, because that was when we moved to Dulwich.

My mental image shows me careering into the pavement when I turned from Roseway into Turney Road. I tumbled to the ground as I tried to master the corner, and my father came running up to disentangle me from the bike, reassuring me that everyone falls off at first.

Trying to unravel these layers of childhood was like choosing photographs for an album. I needed a good balance to tell the story, yet sometimes I had too many images and sometimes only a few. Early memories are naturally sparse, but setting scenes in the first chapter is important, and as the writing progressed more incidents came flooding back.

Everyone remembers his or her own childhood: tricks played at school; a first boy or girl friend; peculiarities of eccentric aunts; a world full of imagination. So the 'I' in *Safe as Houses*, in many ways, could be any small girl growing up in the 1940s. But I had never thought of those growing up years as *history,* until I recently asked a young boy what he knew about the Second World War and he said, 'We don't do history at school.'

Maybe the war, with its bombs and raids, rations and restrictions has slipped into history without my realising it, but it wasn't the only influence on our lives. Attitudes were so different then.

There were no 'teenagers'. Children were children right up to sixteen or seventeen. We then went through a kind of limbo time of being not quite adult until we 'came of age' at twenty-one. Those who grew up then will remember; those who have come since, may find a picture of childhood far different from their own.

As events unfold, I have parallelled happenings in the wider world, to show how they interacted with those of the family and the small girl growing up. But, like all children, my brothers and I used our imaginations in detailed games, for minor details are the essence of life. And through our activities we learnt to override the realities of war and the restrictive years that followed.

'Story' is an incomplete world, because *Safe as Houses* is also a documentary of a child's life through the 1940s and a little beyond. It doesn't simply say, 'This is what I did'. Hopefully, for readers, it will stimulate their own reminders of childhood too.

MS
Christow, Devon 1995

1. Setting Scenes: 1934-1939

In the hot summer of 1939, when war was rapidly approaching, David, Nigel and I went down with ptomaine poisoning. There was talk of a fly or flies in a bottle of milk, which may have been the cause, and we were seriously ill for several days.

But our parents' main concern was to get us well enough to travel. They knew evacuating children to the country was seen as a priority, and that plans had already been drawn up so that if, and then when, war started, children would be ready to move away from built-up areas likely to be bombed. We were living in Herne Hill in South London by then, having moved nearly four years earlier from Marlow in Buckinghamshire, where I had emerged as an unexpected ten-pound bundle; third child and only daughter of Stephen and Lilian Green.

The rise of Hitler and his defiance of the Versailles Treaty had had no meaning for me. His increasing persecution of the Jews, demands on Czechoslovakia and links forged between Germany and Italy were far away. But my parents, like so many others, were deeply concerned by these progressive rumblings of war and where they could lead, while I slept and played contentedly.

One reason for moving from Marlow to Herne Hill had been because of my aunts' school, Glenshee House, at 68 and 149 Half Moon Lane, two old ivy-clad buildings on opposite sides of the road. My mother had started as a pupil-teacher at this PNEU school, when she was sixteen. Afterwards she became the kindergarten mistress and had soon met the tall, handsome brother of the owners.

My father-to-be was in the RAF, so when he returned home on leave he discovered the new kindergarten teacher, and their friendship blossomed. They began their married life in Baildon, Yorkshire, before moving to Shiplake in Oxfordshire where David was born. Nigel came into the world in Marlow nearly three years later, and I arrived only thirteen months after him.

I learned, many years later, that my unexpected birth was

They began their married life in Yorkshire

On holiday in the Isle of Wight

because of an old wives' tale which said breast-feeding prevented conception. So I was probably a bit of a shock arriving like that, with an infected eye that had to be bandaged for several weeks.

I was eleven months old when we had left Marlow and moved temporarily to a flat in Herne Hill. But we soon moved again, this time to a house on the corner of Elmwood Road, just up the hill from Glenshee House School. Coming back to South London meant our mother could return to the kindergarten, David could join the school, and a year later Nigel could also start.

Before it was my turn we went on holiday to the Isle of Wight. My parents hired a beach hut, and with the weather hot and sunny we spent a long happy week playing in the sand and picnicking on the beach, while far away the rumblings of war increased. Soon after we returned from holiday, when I was three, I started in the nursery class at Glenshee House.

Towards the end of my first summer term, I watched eager preparations for sports day. The large back lawn was neatly cut, chairs were set in place, a rostrum was erected for announcements and prize-giving, and parents started to arrive. I sat through the races, watching the older children competing, until the toddlers' race was announced. Then I raced enthusiastically to the winning post. Being far bigger than the other two struggling competitors didn't diminish my pride, when I walked up to the rostrum to collect my prize.

I heard Nigel's name being repeatedly called, for he had won all his races, and by the end of the ceremony I saw him clutching a large collection of small prizes. But once the visiting parents had left and the sports' equipment was being stacked away, Nigel was called to the rostrum again, to see our willowy and commanding aunts, Florence, Madeline and the seldom-seen headmistress, Norah.

'Now, Nigel, you may choose one of your prizes to keep,' said Florence, the eldest aunt. 'The other prizes must be handed back for another time.'

'It wouldn't be good for you to keep them *all*,' agreed Madeline.

Poor Nigel couldn't argue, because when they were together the aunts seemed daunting and strangely 'correct' to us. Each wore her long brown hair pulled back into a tight bun, which gave this 'not to be disobeyed' appearance. But while Auntie Flo's bun was usually neat, wisps of hair escaped from Auntie Madeline's.

Grandma, who lived with the aunts, was shorter and rounder with a quiet voice, gentle smile and another neat bun. She also made us feel we must be careful what we said and must always be on our best behaviour, so Nigel's prizes were handed back.

My father's father had died in 1930, just after David was born, so for me there had only ever been Grandma and the aunts. I felt a peculiar kind of awe when I visited them at number 68, the larger of the two school buildings. As I walked through the side gateway, and on past the school's neat flower garden to confront the impressive Georgian house, this feeling swept over me. Standing on the wide gravel path, I would stare at the immense building, with its regularly spaced windows dominating the ivy-clad walls. In some places I saw only an outline, where a window had been bricked up to reduce a former window tax, but now ivy crept over the blocked-in spaces.

Zig-zagging up to a flat roof on one side of the house climbed an iron fire-escape, and sometimes I looked up at the fretted treads, wondering if I could climb to the top. But I thought I might slip through the open spaces between the steep intimidating steps, so when Nigel dared me I only ventured a little way.

David, at seven or eight, was used to the fire-escape, and one hot sunny day, when he had an urgent message for Mother, he hurried up the steps to a low metal gate at the top, leading to the flat roof. As he reached the gate, two sunbathing, bare-breasted figures, full of confusion, hastily scrambled for decency.

'David, you must *never* come up the fire-escape *unannounced*,' Mother said, reprovingly, as she tried to regain her modesty.

Auntie Madeline, scrabbling for her blouse and completely flustered by her uncharacteristic lapse from conformity, said, 'You should have *knocked!*'

Grandma and the aunts lived in a separate downstairs section of the school, where the decaying plaster of the inner walls was soft to touch and we could hear mice scampering round inside them. And sometimes we found mouse dirts in the kitchen.

On social occasions, only, when we were permitted to cross the impressive main entrance of the old building, I would stand in the high-ceilinged hall, with its magnificent staircase leading to forbidden territory, and I would know I had to be particularly well behaved. Even so, one day when no one was about, Nigel and I crept furtively up the wide polished stairs to the darker polished landing.

We peeped into the first room, where sun slanted over dazzling white bedspreads and spilled on to the floorboards. A white painted locker stood by each iron-framed bed, but there was space for no other furniture. We tiptoed along the landing to the next room and the next, and found similar small dormitories. With the mystery of the forbidden rooms a mystery no more, we crept silently downstairs before we were seen.

'Can we go in yet?' I asked David one Saturday, as I manoeuvred my tricycle over bumpy uncut grass.

'Not yet, they haven't called us,' he said.

'Why can't we go and see what they're doing.' Nigel was impatiently slashing at stinging nettles with a stick.

'Because it's an *important* meeting.' But even David was beginning to think we had been forgotten.

We were playing by a dilapidated summer house, half hidden in a tangle of overgrown grass and weeds. The summer house — once a favourite place to play — was in the garden of number 149, the original school building, but we seldom went there now, for strange things were happening in the grown-up world.

Eventually, David said, 'I think we can go in now.' And he led us across the long grass to the back of the house.

He found a side door leading to a narrow, spiral staircase and started up the steep stairs. I followed behind Nigel, and as I clung hand over hand up the circling central bannisters, I had a feeling of uncertainty, that something was wrong. Ahead of me, David pushed open the door of a small room at the top of the stairs, and voices inside abruptly stopped.

'Go back to the garden. I shall be out in a moment,' I heard Mother say. And when I peered round the door I saw Auntie Flo and Auntie Madeline, unsmiling, looking on. But although it was kept from me, David knew that Auntie Norah had died and the future of the school was being discussed.

Florence — who always wore navy blue — became headmistress, and the school was consolidated at number 68. Auntie Flo, in her neat navy skirt and cardigan, with slightly pointed lace-up shoes, also personally supervised the secretarial training of the senior girls. But my favourite of Father's numerous brothers and sisters was Auntie Madeline.

Madeline — who always wore browns and greens and similar 'sensible shoes' — was in charge of the boarders. She was also Nigel's form mistress and occasionally, when she was on her own with us, she laughed and joked in a less inhibited way. On these days we called her Auntie Madge. We laughed secretly when we heard the aunts calling each other 'Madeline dear' and 'Floey dear'. And it was odd to hear our parents being called 'Stephen dear' and 'Lilian dear' in the same exaggerated voice.

Madeline and Florence

In the long summer holiday, Nigel and I played in our tiny garden and sometimes we opened the side gate and took turns riding our tricycle along the pavement then in through the front gateway. At other times we sat under the branches of an elder bush in the corner of the garden, making pretend 'cigarettes' from the soft dead twigs. And all the while there was a strange feeling of uncertainty in the air; something different was happening.

This didn't really affect me until we were fitted with things called gas masks. Hitler's rising power meant nothing to me; neither did his quickly-broken, repeated claims that he had no territorial demands on Europe. I was oblivious to his annexing of Austria, invasion of Czechoslovakia and threat to Poland, while the Japanese belief in their *Divine Mission* to rule the world, was way beyond my insular world.

But the fear of gas attacks was a substantial worry for adults, and I sensed something was wrong. The Civil Defence and the Local Defence Volunteers (LDV) gave frequent warnings of what to expect and the different types of possible gas — lung, tear, sneezing or mustard. Local identification squads had been set up, and yellow gas-detector paint coated the tops of many letter boxes.

'Can I have a Mickey Mouse one?' I said, when the need for gas masks was encouragingly explained to me.

'We'll see,' said Mother. And we all trooped along to the nearest Air Raid Precautions (ARP) centre.

'Sorry,' said the issuing officer, after we had queued up for our gas masks to be fitted. 'Two to four is the age limit for Mickey Mouse masks. You'd soon grow out of it.'

Although I was still four, I was assured that the black rubber mask, with its celluloid visor, was far more grown-up. So I took off my little round tortoiseshell-framed glasses and stood proudly as one of these extraordinary contraptions was fitted over my head. As soon as we arrived home we tried them on again.

'Listen to this,' said Nigel, blowing hard against the black rubber. 'It makes rude noises!'

Each time I put on my gas mask the rubber crimped my face, the visor steamed up on the inside and the buckle on the strap caught in my hair. Even so, I didn't mind gas mask practice. Seeing how quickly I could put on the rubbery smelling mask, then parading round talking in an echoey voice, that wasn't my own, became an exciting new game. Afterwards I put the mask carefully in its box and hung the carrying cord over my shoulder.

Towards the end of August any hope that war could be averted faded, when the 'wireless' announced that Hitler had signed a non-aggression pact with the Soviet Union. And on the 1st September, news everyone hoped they wouldn't hear, finally came through. Germany had invaded Poland. With this latest invasion, and yet another violation of an earlier non-aggression pact, my parents knew war had become inevitable. Hurriedly they prepared to leave Herne Hill.

Although David, Nigel and I were recovering from ptomaine poisoning, the following morning we trudged down Half Moon Lane to Herne Hill station with our parents. Each clutching our gas mask box and a bag of necessities, we joined a throng of people milling around: voices, cries, pushing and shoving, clattering feet and a babble of noise. Bewildered by the crowds, I queued up with the other children, where a friendly-faced, grey-haired lady pinned a label to my coat, giving my name and destination. I was handed a bag of biscuits and an orange for the journey, before Father herded us towards the platform.

I clung tightly to Mother's hand, staring at the patterns of close-up coats. And filled with mixed feelings of anticipation and unreality, I wondered what was happening. When I heard an electric train rattling into the station, we all moved forward. Doors were thrust open as guard and porters shouted above the noise. I followed David and Nigel and climbed up the steep step into a murky carriage, then I was squashed into a corner by the window.

I watched my parents helping more children into the carriage, and saw tearful farewells of other family groups. But our mother stayed with us, as she was one of the teachers in charge of the evacuees from Glenshee House School. And Father stayed to help on the journey and to see us safely settled in.

At thirty-seven he wasn't in the first age-band of men called up for military service, although my parents knew that if the war persisted, it would not be long before he was. But these worries meant nothing to me.

With shrill blasts from the guard's whistle and distant shouts, the crowded train slowly pulled away from the platform. I caught a glimpse of trees in Brockwell Park and houses slipping by. I listened to the rhythmic drumming of wheels and watched changing scenes flash past, enjoying the seldom-experienced train journey, with no knowledge that we were on our way to Patcham on the outskirts of Brighton.

Surprisingly there was no knowledge, either, that children evacuated to the south coast would be in the flight path of enemy planes, with air attacks and 'dog fights' overhead. Neither was it foreseen that the following year Brighton would be designated an invasion area with restricted entry. So Patcham had become a reception centre for evacuees, and soon we were finding our way to a neat road of terraced houses.

'You and Nigel will be in one house,' Mother explained to David. 'And Margaret and I will be next door. Now you will be very good boys, won't you?' she added, straightening Nigel's grey school cap and unruly tie.

'Where's Daddy going to be?'

'He's got to go back to London. But he'll be down at the weekends when he can.'

'I'll stay here tonight,' Father said. 'And tomorrow we'll explore Patcham.'

I watched as David and Nigel were handed over to an unknown person, then I went with my parents into the adjoining house. As the door closed behind us, I noticed a different sort of smell. All houses had *different* smells, and this particular house had congested, heavy furniture, which made it seem strangely dark. I didn't like being separated in these unknown places, with unknown people, but at least I would be with my mother.

The next morning — Sunday the third of September — we set off for a short walk so we could be together and not in the way of the other two families. We had just reached the top of a sloping field, and were looking out across peaceful countryside, when an unexpected whirring noise startled us. With the rising and falling sound ominously close, we hurried back to the two houses.

I had no idea of the true significance of that wailing air raid siren, even though I sensed that whatever was happening wasn't welcome. But it was a false alarm and all was to remain quiet for several months to come. Later, this period was called the 'phoney war', because the expected air raids didn't happen. But my parents knew it was far from phoney elsewhere, when the wireless reported that German U-boats were attacking shipping, and the S.S. *Athenia,* carrying 1,000 passengers, was torpedoed on its way from Belfast to Montreal. Many merchant and naval ships soon met a similar fate.

By the end of September, Poland's courageous fight had been lost, and Poland was divided into western and eastern halves for Germany and Russia to administer. Meanwhile reports that all around the world members of the British Commonwealth were mobilising ready for action, added some hope to the spiralling gloomy news — but I was unaware of such things.

Instead of the familiar programmes we were used to hearing, the BBC Home Service broadcast gramophone records, or Sandy Macpherson playing the BBC theatre organ. This day-long music, in the unfamiliar house, was regularly interrupted with news bulletins giving the latest war details.

At meal times I heard the background drone of the news, but I didn't listen, because while I sat at the table I watched the man of the house mixing his custard and gravy together! I was fascinated by the peculiar habit and had no idea why he did it, but he was a grumpy man who seldom spoke, so I eyed him cautiously and hoped he wouldn't notice me.

The *News* also gave details of the RAF bombing German warships and harbours, while the Royal Navy depth-charged U-boats in an attempt to stop the rising losses. But watching the grumpy man, hunched over his food in that small dark room, and coping with my new surroundings were always more important.

Even worse than the grumpy man was the blackout. Every evening, as soon as it started to get dark, I saw the windows being covered with thick curtains or specially made blackout material.

'Put that light out!' wardens or policemen would shout, if a chink of light escaped.

When I peeped through the curtains I saw no street lights and few cars, with only a pin-prick beam showing through their masked headlights. Occasionally the moon shone on the recently painted white lines down the centre of the road and along the edges of the pavements. But although we were prepared for raids, no raids came.

Our parents hated evacuation and being separated as we were, but they still felt that London would soon be bombed. Going back was out of the question, even though they wanted us all to be together. So one weekend, when Father came down to see us, they began discussing the possibility of giving up our house in Herne Hill.

While they were in the small dark sitting room, talking over what needed to be done, I was in the back garden playing. I looked up from my intricate game to see a dark-haired boy grinning at me. I knew he lived up the road, so I didn't mind when he took my hand and led me into the garden basement room, crowded with deck chairs, cobwebs and garden litter. But I didn't like it when he told me to take down my knickers.

'It's only a game,' he said, reassuringly.

The boy looked even older than David, so I was afraid to say no. Smiling, he added, 'You can have a sweet.'

I looked longingly at the sweet, until I heard familiar voices outside.

'Margaret. Margaret, where are you?' The garden door opened, and there were my parents hurrying towards me. I realised by their reaction that something was wrong, and when I was questioned afterwards I was told *never* to go in the basement room again.

But we left Patcham soon afterwards, and in the cold snowbound winter of 1939 we moved to Wiltshire, where 'war' gradually took on a new meaning for me.

2. They Wouldn't Bomb Our Little School: Wiltshire 1939-1941

We moved to the small village of Purton not far from Swindon, where Father became manager of the local British Home Stores (BHS). He had formerly worked for British Industries Fair, but now there was a war, British industry no longer needed the same promotion. As soon as we arrived, he bought a large 28-inch-wheel bicycle from Webbers the cycle shop, to ride along the country lanes to Swindon each day.

Webbers was in the centre of the village, opposite a road to the village school and the neighbouring village of Wooton Bassett. From the shop, Station Road led down to a narrow bridge over the railway line, and as we walked towards it tall terraced houses seemed to peer down at me from either side. Sometimes, when we heard a train snorting in the distance, Nigel and I ran on ahead to wait near the bridge. We would see the smudge of smoke, before the big engine chugged into view and we could wave to the driver.

Before reaching the bridge, Witts Lane turned off the main street, winding its way to a field, and a little way along, on the left-hand side, a small development of detached houses had sprung up, called Jubilee Estate. Here, gradually, I started to notice the effects of war.

I was five by the time we moved to Purton and ready to start at Purton Infants' School. Each morning, with David and Nigel always ahead of us, Mother and I climbed the wide gravel driveway, making our way up to the squat grey-stone building.

'Is there an air raid shelter for the children to go to?' Mother had asked, on our first visit.

'Oh, they wouldn't bomb *our* little school!' the headmistress said, naively.

'Our little school' wouldn't be a deliberate target, we knew that, but when an air raid warning sounded, bombing wasn't accurate, so no one knew where bombs would fall. And without realising it, we had moved to a front-line centre of war factories and airfields, as the area was later described. Civilian airfields in the district, like all airfields, had been taken over for military use. So, too, had the many engineering firms, while Swindon's well-equipped railway workshops added to the munitions' output, in addition to their engine repair and construction work. But we had no idea; neither, it seemed, had the enemy.

Not long after we moved to Purton, the first heavy flakes of winter snow began to settle. Trudging to school one morning, with David, Nigel and our mother, my black booted feet sank into the soft white folds. Ahead of us, we could see a bus that had slewed sideways into a fence on the ice-packed surface of Witts Lane, blocking the narrow road.

To get past seemed impossible, but the boys — who as usual had run on in front — climbed the snow-covered fence and over the bonnet of the bus to the other side. But I plodded home with Mother.

I accepted my new school, the different house and living in a small village, because everything to me was immediate. I even accepted the road block set up across the bridge and manned by soldiers. But I was surprised one day to see our large zinc bath standing majestically in the dining room. And I was even more surprised when neighbours came round with pots, pans and all kinds of kitchen utensils, which they threw into the bath.

'What's it for?' I asked, as the strange collection grew.

'To make more aeroplanes,' explained Mother. 'To help win the war.'

How do you make an aeroplane out of a saucepan? I wondered.

As soon as the bath was full, I heard an old lorry rumbling down the road and watched the pots and pans being piled into the back. I didn't know the lorry emptied out its load at a nearby government depot, ready to go to factories to be re-used in another form, or that Mother had heard a radio appeal by Lady Reading, head of the Woman's Voluntary Service (WVS). I just knew it was part of this thing called 'war'.

Through the appeal, Lord Beaverbrook, the Minister of Aircraft Production, had asked for aluminium to turn into fighter planes, so Mother had immediately put our old zinc bath into use as a collection point. After two months, when the special appeal ended, we heard that a thousand tons of metal had been collected. Later, I saw iron railings around parks and gardens being uprooted, to be used for making steel towards 'the war effort'. But the significance of it all eluded me, so collecting pots and pans in the old bath in the dining room became normal.

I knew food was short and that rationing began while we were in Purton, because I saw the ration books — green for children and buff for adults. They had been distributed in October 1939, when we were registered and issued with our identity cards, but rationing had been delayed until January. To begin with, bacon, ham, butter and sugar were the only rationed goods. Then meat, tea, cheese and jam were included; later still came a 'points system' for tinned goods. But it hardly affected me. I just ate the meals provided.

One morning, when David, Nigel and I were playing in the front garden, we heard sounds of boys coming noisily along the road. Seeing the three of us, they stopped and leant over the gate. But to my surprise they started jeering and shouting at us.

'Don't take any notice,' muttered David, trying not to see them.

But we stopped playing as a putrefied potato exploded at our feet, and suddenly we were being bombarded with more rotting potatoes. For a moment we stood there as they splattered to the ground. Then one by one David and Nigel picked up the slimy, squashed missiles and hurled them back. I threw some too, not noticing the disgusting smell on my hands and clothes. Throwing back the potatoes was far more urgent.

While we waged our own grubby war, fierce battles were raging in the wider world. In February and March, under the pretext of strengthening her boundaries, Russia had bombed Finnish oil depots before annexing the country's eastern borders. Early April saw ruthless German bombing with the invasion of Denmark and Norway, and in May they overran Holland, Belgium and Luxembourg. That was the day, in Britain, when Winston Churchill took over as Prime Minister from Neville Chamberlain.

Four days later Rotterdam was blitzed, and all the while refugees poured on to the roads, trying to escape the bombing and inevitable terror of invading armies. Our solid brown Bakelite wireless set gave regular reports, and I saw my parents in the dining room listening to the alarming news: German armies continuing their surge forward, fighting their way into northern

France; retreating allied troops pouring into Dunkirk; thousands of soldiers being brought off the beaches; a flotilla of small seaworthy boats chugging across the channel to join in the rescue.

The German advance using Blitzkrieg tactics must have seemed unstoppable, to my parents, with Britain next in line. Yet, war or no war, life at home had to continue as normally as possible, and, with little knowledge of the intricacies of war, I played in the garden whenever I could.

One bright sunny afternoon, Father decided we should all cycle to Wooton Bassett as an 'outing'. On the back of his large bicycle he had fixed a metal seat for me, so I was

Life continued as normally as possible

carried along the narrow country lanes, enjoying the headyscent of meadowsweet and flowering privet. I clung tightly to his shirt, feeling a faint breeze brushing my face and catching my hair, but my little round glasses saved the summer insects from flying into my eyes, each time I peeped round to see where we were going.

David had a new bike from Webbers the cycle shop, too, so he sped on ahead, with Nigel pedalling furiously behind him on a far-too-small 'fairy cycle'. Mother had managed to borrow an old-fashioned dark-brown bicycle, with huge wheels and a guard to prevent skirts from getting entangled in the spokes, and in this motley fashion we straggled along the lanes.

There was no need to cycle in single file, for there was unlikely to be any traffic. Petrol was in such short supply that we had heard of gas-powered cars, with huge balloons of gas on the roof, and of buses towing mobile gas-making contraptions. But here, in Purton, cycling or walking were far more practical — and usually more fun.

Mother, who wasn't used to cycling, valiantly tried to master her unwieldy machine, but she was gradually trailing behind. As each twist in the lane hid her from view, I repeatedly looked round to see where she was. At one moment, when we all looked back, she wobbled wildly round the corner, lurched sideways and toppled into the ditch at the side of the road. Hurriedly we cycled back to see if she was hurt. But the sight of the large brown bicycle bedecked with brambles, and Mother emerging from the ditch, started us laughing. Mother, shaken by her fall, didn't see the funny side, and sadly the cycle ride ended.

Beyond our little world, Germany had swept on through France, leaving a wake of ruined towns and villages and a flood of refugees fleeing from the advancing army. My parents were still glued to the wireless for each bulletin, discussing the news in detail. Although I didn't listen, it went on around me and I continued to sense all was not well.

When Italy, under Mussolini, declared war on Britain and France another blow was struck. Three days later, after heavy German bombing, Paris fell. With over half France now under German rule the position looked grim, and everyone expected Britain to be the next target. So when the Channel Islands were quietly taken over in July this was seen as the first move.

Training for the ARP, LDV and AFS (Auxiliary Fire Service) was stepped up, and we heard tales of lorry loads of sand bags stacked in front of doorways and against windows of essential buildings. Camouflaged concrete 'pill boxes' had already been built in strategic places to house machine guns, and sand-bagged wardens' posts suddenly appeared.

Father had become an air raid warden as soon as we arrived in Purton, so Nigel, proudly wearing the warden's helmet and carrying stirrup pump and hose pipe, sat on Pegasus our rocking horse and became a 'warden' too.

Searchlights, gun batteries and barrage balloons had all been deployed in readiness for defence, while anti-tank

Nigel became a warden too

trenches were dug and road blocks set in place. And we saw signposts and road and station names being hurriedly taken down to confuse the expected enemy troops. Each shattering news bulletin brought them nearer, as their surge forward became more threatening. Then Hitler issued 'invasion dates' — a new date being announced each time one passed with no troops landing.

'He's trying to break the British spirit,' I heard Father say, as he scanned through the *Daily Telegraph*, another vital source of news.

'He'll never succeed!' said Mother, vehemently.

I didn't realise their feelings were always on a see-saw. But they knew the Luftwaffe had switched to the next phase of the onslaught, with mass day and night raids on London. And, in return, they knew the RAF bombed Berlin, German harbours and coastal gun emplacements and the concentration of barges waiting to invade.

When I heard them cheering and saw their spirits rise, I had only a vague idea about British planes inflicting heavier losses on German bombers and fighters. But if my parents were jubilant then so was I, and I could immerse myself in games.

Sometimes, when we played in the field at the end of Witts Lane, I picked bunches of bright yellow buttercups. Nigel and I 'sold' them in the shop we set up in the garden. We also picked giant wild parsley stalks to sell as rhubarb. When we moved to an

Picking flowers for our 'shop'

unfinished development in nearby Swindon, we continued our shop by 'borrowing' bricks and planks of wood from the building site. We dragged the planks home and rested them on the bricks to make a counter for a *real* shop, where we sold packets of jelly and 1d Oxo cubes we acquired from the larder.

Our move to Fitzroy Road in Swindon, happened during the summer holidays in 1940, when I was nearly six, Nigel seven and David almost ten. The house was part of a small development on the southern edge of Old Swindon, a mile or so from Wroughton Aerodrome.

As the boys and I looked at the rough, earthy ground of the unmade garden, we talked about making our own town in the same way that buildings and roads were growing around us. Standing there, I imagined it transformed with roads and houses, shops and schools. Although this was a wild dream, seeds were sown in our minds and slowly, very slowly, they started to germinate. But it was to take over two years before that first hint of fantasy began to bear fruit.

In the meantime we played on the half-finished building site. We weren't supposed to be there, but wood, bricks and builder's litter had been abandoned when all able-bodied men had been called up for military service, or were needed for 'war work'. And the mounds of earth with planks to balance along, the inviting foundations and empty houses were far too tempting to be ignored.

'If I tell you something,' said Nigel, one day, when he and I had gone into a partly finished house to examine the rough-bricked rooms. 'If I tell you something, you've got to promise not to tell anyone.'

'All right. What is it?'

'You promise? You won't tell *anyone?*'

'Yes, I *promise*. What is it?'

'I'm going to run away!'

'Run away?' I repeated.

'I'm going to hide in one of these empty houses. And you can bring me food every day.'

I stared at him. 'Yes, but. . .'

'But you're not to tell anyone. You promised.'

For several days we talked secretly about his plans. I couldn't think why he wanted to run away and I didn't want him to go, but Nigel continued planning — what he would take with him, when he would go, how long he would stay away — while I worried about what I should have to do.

The worst part would be going alone to the building site. Supposing someone saw me taking food? Supposing they asked where Nigel was? How could I tell them when I had promised not to? It was a big problem for a six-year-old, but fortunately the days slipped by and Nigel changed his mind. He soon forgot his elaborate plans as some other unlikely scheme took root — and the war escalated.

I realised the news was serious by my parents' reaction, but I didn't understand that Japan had signed a tripartite agreement with Germany and Italy. The agreement ensured that the Japanese respected the right of Germany to 'establish a new order' in Europe, while Japan was poised to 'establish a new order' in the Far East. But it also strengthened Hitler's determination to invade Britain and win the war by Christmas.

With Hitler's supposed victory in sight, the incessant fire-raising raids on London continued. So, too, did the attacks on coastal towns and Allied shipping. One tragedy reported in a radio talk given by King George VI, was the torpedoing of the evacuation ship, *City of Benares*, with the loss of seventy-three children on their way to Canada — but that news was kept from me.

Tucked away in Swindon, with the frequent roar of British planes, but only a few air raids, we heard the harrowing news bulletins continue. By now they were no longer surrounded by light music or the theatre organ, for to help raise morale familiar programmes began to creep back.

I was conscious of the programmes issuing from the wireless: ITMA, or *It's That Man Again*, with Tommy Handley and innumerable catch phrases by outrageous characters; *Monday Night at Eight*; *Henry Hall's Guest Night* and a host of others, although I didn't really listen to them. But the laughter made life seem normal, and I heard my parents joining in their favourite *Any Questions?* and *The Brains Trust*, answering questions when they could or disputing the teams' opinions. During the day, many appeals urging listeners to greater economy, efficiency and factory production, added a more serious note.

So, like everyone else, we coped with daily life, extending our meagre rations, saving aluminium, old clothes, jam jars, bones, paper and pig food. Local authorities collected the separated waste, and from time to time came the special drives for one particular item. I saw posters showing how salvage was used — milk tops made aeroplanes; rubber made paratroopers' boots; bones made cordite for cartridges. But they were just pictures to me.

That autumn term, David and Nigel started at Lethbridge Road Junior School and I joined the infants. Each morning Mother walked with us up the long road of tall terraced houses. At the far end, dominating the road, towered the old Victorian junior school, with its high windows staring down at us like all-seeing eyes. To the right stood a wooden single-storey building for the infants.

Mother left me at the infants' gateway, and I skirted a tiny pond surrounded by flat stone slabs. As I sidled past, from the corner of my eye I watched a boy — fat and self confident — jumping from side to side over the pond weed. I tried not to be noticed but he always teased me, that boy, although I never knew his name.

In the mornings we did reading and number work and drew pictures. In the afternoons construction toys and jigsaws were handed round, and on certain days we were given multicoloured blobs of tangy Plasticine, with large Plasticine-splattered boards. But for me there was always uncertainty; the uncertainty of not knowing what to do, yet not daring to ask.

When the first notes of an air raid warning started up, we left our work and were quickly hustled from the classroom to line up by the pond. Our small wooden building had no suitable shelter, so we were led in an orderly 'crocodile' to Avenue Road, an adjoining road of houses with low walls enclosing tiny gardens.

Before the warning, we had been told to knock on a front door and ask to be taken in while the air raid lasted. But now it was actually sounding, the thought of opening a gate, walking up a strange garden path and knocking on an unknown door terrified me. I stood by a closed gate, lost and afraid; afraid to open it; afraid to move as the road slowly emptied of children. The fear of meeting strange people was far greater than the threat of bombs and enemy planes.

Eventually, when my form teacher saw me still standing there, she took me up the path, knocked on the door and handed me over to a kindly person; a sudden sense of warmth and protection flooded through me. I was safe once more.

One morning, as we walked up Lethbridge Road to school, we saw an elderly workman boarding up the front of a house. A gaping hole where the window had been, exposed the stark contents of the living room.

'What's happened?'

'Did we have a raid?'

We hurried on to school where everyone was talking about the damage. I soon learned that the milkman's horse had charged up the road and in sudden fright crashed through the small front garden. It had continued its charge through the front room window, scattering milk as it dragged the milk cart behind. I had a nasty, uneasy feeling each morning, as I walked past the house where the poor frightened horse had died, and always looked across to the other side of the road, rather than see the boarded house front. But the memory lingered with me.

Christmas was nearing, the second Christmas of the war, when the flat roof on the bedroom above the garage suddenly started to leak. No one knew why, but it meant the bedroom couldn't be used.

'The children will just have to be in one room, until it's mended,' I heard Mother say. So our three beds were pushed together in one small bedroom. But I didn't mind, it was cosy and warm and I could listen to the boys talking.

As I opened my eyes on Christmas morning I could hear them, but there were no expected sounds of rustling paper; no voices saying 'Look what I've got.' I slid my feet down the bed to feel for the weight of a bulky stocking. This way and that way went my toes, but the stocking wasn't there. Suddenly, amidst laughter and apologies, Mother hurried in with the forgotten stockings. She handed them round as I joined in the laughter, and with a strange mixture of feelings I told myself I hadn't really believed in Father Christmas anyway.

Early in the new year, I realised our stay in Swindon was coming to an end when Father was appointed manager of the newly-built BHS in Swansea. He had to return there to arrange housing for us, and as he was leaving I whispered to him in a small, reluctant voice:

'Will you get a house that doesn't have big windows?'

'Why don't you like big windows?' he said, in surprise.

'I don't want the Germans to look in and see us!' This was my greatest fear.

The day Father returned from his reconnaissance, we were sitting round the kitchen table having tea. I was listening to the boiler popping and spluttering in the corner, sending its warmth into the room, when the key clicked in the front door lock. We jumped to our feet to rush into the hall to meet him. But before running after the others, I stopped long enough to spread thick butter and fish paste on my slice of bread. The yellow pat and the pot of salmon and shrimp paste were far too tempting, even though I knew precious rationed butter had to be scraped on.

That icy February, David, Nigel and I were in the midst of chicken-pox, when we moved to Sketty on the western outskirts of Swansea. Father had managed to hire a Morris 8, so we were bundled inside with cases, packages and over-night things squashed around us.

But when we arrived in the evening after our long, bumpy journey, we found our rented house in Eversley Road locked, and there was no way of getting the key. Father drove us round to see Mr and Mrs Jones, the couple he had stayed with while he was house-hunting, and kindly they made room for us all. The next day we bundled back into the car and found our way to our new home.

As I climbed out of the car, I stared at the substantial semi-detached house. It was built on a hill, so the front had two floors while the back had three. I had never seen a house on different levels before. The lowest level, which was immediately named the Underworld, would make a wonderful place to play.

I didn't know then that the space under the stairs in the Underworld was soon to become our much-used air raid shelter.

3. Down in the Underworld: Swansea 1941-1942

Our Swansea house, with its sturdy walls and high ceilings, appeared ancient to me compared with the newly-built house in Swindon. But the greatest disappointment was the large sash windows. Deep round bays for the sitting room and main bedroom, and tall tinted windows in the bathroom and hall, dominated the front of the house. While at the back large square bays overlooked Singleton Park beyond the Gower Road.

How could my father choose a house with big windows, I thought, when I had asked him not to? I didn't say this to my parents, although they must have guessed something was wrong.

'There's nothing to worry about,' Mother assured me. 'We're going to put blackout material up to all the windows. Anyway, no one can see inside.'

I wasn't totally convinced, but as I looked across the back lawn, other thoughts quickly took over. The narrow garden seemed large to me, falling away to a tiny piece of rough ground. And when the boys and I struggled into our boots to investigate, we found that it led to a path between houses down to the Gower Road, opposite the entrance to Singleton Park.

The piece of rough ground, we noticed, was no more than the ends of three gardens, giving access to two brick sheds. It bordered the gardens of Mr and Mrs Evans — our next door neighbours — and the Dovey family beyond them, so David gave it the grand name of 'Dovans Field'. In the summer David would mow this piece of grass to make a perfect place to play, but now it was February with more urgent things to do.

First priorities were to fix blackout material to all the windows and to find a suitable place for a shelter. Being underground, the front half of the Underworld was ideal — particularly under the narrow stairs that led down from the hall. A lavatory led off this front section, while in the lighter back half was an earthenware sink and a door that led to the garden. Father fixed up a flex and dim light bulb under the stairs, and squashed a single mattress into the space. But I felt doubly safe because of the useful 'escape route' out through to the garden.

Before we arrived, Swansea had experienced many raids, when the busy docks acted as a magnet for German bombers, but there had been a two-months' lull when Coventry, Birmingham and Southampton received the full onslaught of Hitler's bombs. In January the intense bombing had switched to Portsmouth and Plymouth — and all the while we knew London was being blitzed.

Raids on Swansea resumed in January, too, followed by another lull. And during this lull we moved to Eversley Road.

On Wednesday 19th February — with cases and boxes still waiting to be unpacked — the rising drone of an air raid warning jerked me awake. I heard Mother running up stairs calling to Nigel and me, so I scrambled out of bed and pulled on my dressing gown and slippers. I hurried down the stairs, listening to distant bursts of anti-aircraft guns. Nigel was ahead of me as we all converged on a small door in the hall, then made our way down the dark, narrow staircase to the Underworld. The regular pom, pom, pom of anti-aircraft guns was getting louder, with the added muffled throb of German bombers, as we crawled into our shelter.

I settled myself on the mattress, pulling a blanket round me, and studied the upside-down stairs level with my eyes. Halfway along one stair I saw a knot of grainy wood. I looked to see if the other stairs had them, while the outward signs of the raid increased. With the throb of planes came bursting shells, screeching bombs and the shrill of a warden's whistle. But it was cosy in the cramped cupboard and I had no knowledge of the parachute flares that hung in the sky, lighting up the area for the 'baskets' of incendiary bombs that instantly followed; then high explosives rained down. When the flares subsided, searchlights criss-crossed the sky, picking out bright specks of enemy planes.

While the crazy world raged outside we huddled under our blankets. Sometimes we felt the whole house vibrate and heard windows rattling. Sometimes I shut my eyes tightly and held my hands over my ears, or buried my head under a pillow to shut out a particularly loud screech and the crump that followed. I was beginning to get used to the unnerving sounds when, without even a warning flicker, we found ourselves in darkness.

'What's happened?' said Nigel.

'Don't worry, we've got candles.' Mother's voice was reassuring. 'We'll soon have some light.'

I heard a match strike and saw hesitant shadows darting over the walls; weird shapes appeared as heads and hands moved. In the restricted light, I watched greasy stalactites lengthening down each candle. An ARP warden called down the stairs to see if we were all right, and having assured him we were, someone started to sing:

'Ten green bottles hanging on the wall.' So we all joined in.

Slowly, gradually, the throbbing banging world grew quieter, and after nearly five hours of the raid, Father went off to the kitchen to make drinks. Soon a mug of hot cocoa was passed along the line to me, with a biscuit from our tin of emergency rations.

'I spy with my little eye. . .' Mother started, while we waited for the welcome note of 'all-clear'. And we sang 'She'll be Coming Round the Mountain' and 'The Quartermaster's Stores'. When the sound of the all-clear broke through our singing, I felt the tension easing, secure in our semi-underground protection. But the next night the pattern was the same; and the next night, too.

Each morning, as we emerged into a calm new day, news filtered through of more damage and destruction, more buildings shattered, more people killed. And each morning we wondered how long the raids would continue. By Saturday the centre of Swansea had been devastated — and with it the newly completed British Home Stores. Fires still smouldered throughout the area, and unexploded bombs were cordoned off barring the way. Buildings had been opened up like dolls' houses, with furniture tumbled inside. Many more were reduced to rubble.

But that night, when 7.30 approached and we waited for the warning to blare again, no planes came. Swansea's ordeal was temporarily over.

We soon learned that many sewers, drains, gas mains, electric cables and water pipes had been damaged or destroyed. Rescuing victims had been hindered by unexploded bombs, and dangerously damaged buildings created further chaos. Damaged water pipes enabled fires to rage out of control, despite tremendous efforts by fire fighters trying to negotiate hazardous streets. Added to this, at 10 o'clock on the third night, essential communications had been cut when the telephone system went out of action.

The centre of Swansea had been destroyed (SCA)

But soon neighbouring water authorities were sending in tankers and water carts, for distributing water to areas that were completely without.

'Listen,' said David, as he and I stood in the tiny front garden. And I heard the distant crackle of a loudspeaker van getting nearer.

'What's it saying?'

'Something about boiling water before we use it. And there're stand-pipes in the roads for houses that haven't got any.'

'What are stand-pipes?'

But David was already hurrying indoors with the news.

With the town's shopping centre demolished, and many shops on the outskirts inaccessible through fire damage and unexploded bombs, we heard of food convoys bringing food to the homeless at outlying communal centres. And all the time we knew that while Swansea was trying to creep back to normal, London was still being bombed.

Like other towns that had experienced a blitz, Swansea now had a respite, with time to start on the task of clearing up the mess — getting essential services running, housing the homeless and trying to create a pretence at normal life. The BHS needed a temporary home. People needed to get back to work and customers needed something to buy, even if there was little choice.

After the three-night blitz, David, Nigel and I began to settle into a different way of life when we joined our new schools. At first

Mother took us, past the high railings of Singleton Park, down Llythrid Avenue and on through Brynmill Park, then up a short hill and along to our schools.

When we knew the way David was put in charge, and Nigel and I were told we must always do what he said. So we set off on the long trek each morning. As we left Brynmill Park, the wonderful smell of new bread drew us irresistibly towards a bakery in one of the tall terraced houses further up the hill. If there was time, we looked down into the semi-basement watching the dough being pounded into bread, and sometimes we saw an old woman coming out of the house and piling hot loaves into a dilapidated black pram. As she trundled the pram up the road to deliver the loaves to local houses, we ran on to school, still smelling the delicious smell of new bread.

Brynmill Infants' School, solid and old-fashioned with more big windows, was a little further on from the bakery. Through the railings above a rising wall, I could see the asphalt playground that seemed to wrap around one corner of the building, and I worked out the words 'BOYS' and 'GIRLS' carved into concrete slabs above the outside lavatories. David and Nigel left me at the gate and walked up Trafalgar Place to the Junior school — another large old building enclosed by high railings.

While I waited in the playground for the door to open, I watched daring infants climbing along the wall, clutching the railings one hand over the other as the wall grew steadily higher. Once I tried, grasping the spiky railings as my feet edged over the smooth bricks. It was scary looking down so I only progressed a little way.

They spoke differently here in Swansea, faster too, and occasionally I heard a strange language which baffled me. Sometimes this made it harder to fit in, especially as *school,* to me, meant always being 'the new girl'. Even so, as I sat up to a big wooden desk looking through my Beacon reader, I suddenly realised that the words under one of the pictures were actually saying what was happening. It was something to do with Rover the dog seeing John in the tree, and I turned the page to see if the next picture did the same thing.

'Eat up,' said Mother, the next morning, as I struggled through my usual morning porridge, liberally sprinkled with Bemax to give me energy. 'You'll be late for school.'

She was listening to *Kitchen Front* on the wireless and I heard the Radio Doctor saying something about his old friend the dandelion leaf to include in salads, and stinging nettles as an alternative to spinach. I was only half listening, as I swished at flecks of Bemax that floated on the surface of the milky porridge, and I wondered what Rover the dog would do today.

Eventually, with porridge bowls scraped clean, David, Nigel and I set off for school. We were part-way through Brynmill Park on that bright, crisp morning, when the familiar wailing of an air raid siren suddenly erupted.

'What shall we do?' I looked to David for guidance.

'We'll have to keep going,' he said. 'It's too far to go back now.'

With the ominous sound rising and falling, we hurried on through the empty park, wondering why there should be a daytime warning. We had almost reached the swings on the far side when we saw the glinting speck of a plane, low down on the horizon and seemingly coming straight for us.

'Into the bushes!' yelled David, as the throbbing engine grew louder.

We dived behind an ornamental shrub and crouched on the soft earth under the scanty protection of leaves. I covered my head with my hands, trying not to be seen as the plane swept over us.

'Look at that!' said Nigel. 'I can see the markings.'

But I wasn't looking.

We stayed crouching there until we were sure there were no planes following, then David crawled out and checked the sky. 'Come on we can go now,' he said.

I could hardly keep up with the boys as we charged past the bare oak spreading above the swings, my satchel and gas mask banging at my side. On through the gateway hurried my six-year-old legs, struggling up the short hill — with no time to stop at the bakery — then along and down to my school. Here David and Nigel left me as they ran up Trafalgar Place together.

I darted across the playground and a teacher opened the door to let me in. The air raid alert was still on, so she took me straight to the 'shelter', a dimly-lit, cramped cupboard shelved with toys and equipment. Squashed in the aisle between shelves and other children, I wasn't sure whether to play with the toys, so I just stood there, regaining my breath and thinking of the swooping plane I had hidden from.

Further afield the fighting raged on. I had known nothing of the

Italians' invasion of Albania at the start of the war, or that they had moved outwards, with North Africa and then Greece as their objectives. So it meant nothing to me when Greece briefly survived with British and Commonwealth help, until Germany added her weight to the battle.

I heard the names Benghazi, Sidi Barrani, Tobruk, Derna and El Alamein, each time my parents discussed the intense desert fighting. I also heard talk of Wavell, Rommel and Montgomery. But I had no idea of the importance of stopping the Italian and German advance along the North African coast, or that the Suez Canal with its indispensable shipping links, and the Middle East oil fields could be in danger.

Although all this was remote from 'my war', I heard my parents talking earnestly about a BBC appeal for photographs of North Africa. And I saw Father at the dining room table, carefully sorting through his albums of aerial photos he had taken when he was stationed in Egypt before the war. 'If I can't get back in the RAF,' I heard him say, 'at least my photos can be useful.'

'I didn't know you had *flat feet* with all the running you used to do,' said Mother.

'I'm surprised it stopped me getting back in the Air Force.'

But as I listened, I was glad he couldn't get back in, whatever the reason.

The wireless, meanwhile, reported that the Luftwaffe had concentrated its attention on more British industrial towns and ports, with Clydeside and Merseyside being heavily bombed. Cardiff, Glasgow, Birmingham and Bristol did not escape either, and once more Portsmouth was bombarded.

The Minister of Food, Lord Woolton, suggested that tinned food should be saved for 'iron rations' in case of emergency, which had a foreboding sound to me. At the same time we heard that food from Canada and America was becoming increasingly short. During March and April, although no details were announced, 225 loaded ships crossing the Atlantic were sunk by German U-boats and by long-range bombers operating from bases in Norway and France. But with a similar all-out attack on the attackers, the Navy and RAF enabled at least some cargoes to reach bombed British ports. Even so, many foods could not get through.

The picture frieze of bananas around the walls of the green-grocers puzzled me. 'Why do they have pictures of bananas,' I said, 'if they don't sell them?' But no one told me.

When scarce food did appear in shops, I saw long queues forming along the pavement, for queuing had become normal. 'It's amazing,' said Mother. 'If there are queues, people immediately join them.'

I noticed we joined them too, and sometimes, while we waited to be served, I watched the shopkeeper handing someone a mysterious, wrapped package and talking like a ventriloquist.

'Why's he talking in a sideways voice?' I whispered to Mother. I didn't realise scarce items were kept 'under the counter' and saved for regular customers, or that occasionally we also were given mysterious packages.

The Black Market with its vaguely sinister sound was another mystery to me. What was it? I wondered.

'It undermines the whole rationing system,' I heard my parents say. 'It will create even greater shortages. More things will be unobtainable.' And they became increasingly annoyed when they heard of Black Marketeers 'letting down the country'.

To make our own food go further, Mother had already started collecting some of the free leaflets issued by the Ministry of Food. *Puddings Without Eggs; Fruit Bottling Without Sugar; Hedgerow Harvest*; and *Making the Most of the Fat Ration* enabled her to create all kinds of intriguing dishes. A 'butter extender' showed how to eke out the meagre 4-ounce ration by mixing margarine with an equal quantity of cold mashed potato — although we were glad she didn't try it.

For 6d Mother bought *The McDougall's Wartime Cookery Book*. It had a section on unrationed meat dishes using pig's trotters, rabbit, cow heel and sheep's head to supplement the 1s 2d weekly meat ration. But we preferred 'Woolton Pie', made from a mixture of home-grown vegetables, rolled oats and yeast extract instead of meat.

Dripping cake was my favourite for tea, especially when it was made with dried egg powder. We seldom used our sparse ration of fresh eggs for cooking, as these made a main meal, so we grew to like reconstituted egg powder. Some mornings Mother mixed it with a little water and fried the rubbery yellow pancakes for breakfast. We also grew to like raspberry jam made from coloured and flavoured marrow, with wooden 'pips' added to give the appearance of fruit.

'Save bread and you save lives; serve potatoes and you serve your country.' David read out the slogan on the back of a bus, as we walked to school one morning.

I wasn't sure what it meant, but I knew it had something to do with not wasting food, because I wasn't allowed to waste any of mine. And I remembered hearing my parents talking about a woman who had been fined £10 with 2 guineas cost, for feeding bread to the birds. 'Why didn't she put the bread in the pig bin?' I had asked.

Pig food, we were told, helped with the battle for economy, so each day we dropped our own peelings — and very occasional scraps — into the large galvanised container near the corner of the road. As we lifted the lid a putrid smell rose from the nauseating mixture, before the lid could be closed to keep out the flies.

Some days on our way back from school David, Nigel and I wandered through hastily dug wartime allotments. We passed rows of runner beans curling anti-clockwise up their canes, and I noticed a mixed smell of strong aromatic weeds and damp cabbage, whatever the weather. I had heard that the allotments were all part of the Dig for Victory Campaign, and I knew that even the tiniest patch of garden now grew vegetables.

Large areas of parks and commons were also being dug to grow food, and every week I saw my parents listening eagerly to 'The Radio Allotment', transmitted from a piece of waste ground near Broadcasting House. And I saw 'Garden Front' leaflets, giving hints on how to grow and use the produce, although I didn't actually read them.

'I want to be in the Land Army,' I announced one day, after I had seen land girls in corduroy breeches and khaki shirts. 'I could dig for victory and bring in the harvest like they do!'

I knew my cousin Audrey was

My cousin Audrey was a landgirl

a land girl, Grandma and the aunts had written to tell us when they sent news of Uncle John — Father's eldest brother — and his family.

'*Dears all*,' Father would say, in an 'Auntie Flo' or 'Auntie Madeline' voice, when he read out their letters.

But through them we heard news of Father's youngest sister, Agnes, and her family in Newcastle, and of Uncle Keith, the youngest brother, who had gone into the army to work in the War Office when war had started. So in this way we all kept in touch.

'Steve! Steve, did you hear that? Germany has invaded *Russia*,' Mother called from the dining room.

I was staring out of the window across the garden to Singleton Park, as she listened to the unexpected news on the wireless.

'That means Russia is on our side now,' she added, in astonishment, as Father hurried in to hear the latest bulletin.

Although this created yet another 'front' for the Germans to fight, it also spread our munitions even more thinly, for Russia needed tanks and ammunition. But even though the worsening war news looked grim, there was always a 'try to look on the bright side' attitude which helped us carry on, shrugging off inconvenience wherever we could.

I could hardly remember pre-war days when no bombs fell and no air raids jarred my sleep. So I lived for the moment, accepting it all as part of everyday, like going to school, playing in the garden or Dovans Field. And sometimes I went with David and Nigel to Singleton Park.

I liked Singleton Park with its wide open spaces, tall trees and bushes and a strange ring of prehistoric stones to run round. But there were always signs of war. When we walked through the massive gateway, we started down a long drive and passed a gently-sloping, grassy bank. Here, from the corner of my eye, I saw soldiers, sailors and airmen with their wives or girlfriends. I glimpsed them all with a mixture of surprise and sadness. Some stood, some sat and some were lying down; some talked, some laughed but many were crying. I had no idea of the heartache of those partings, but I had been told to walk quickly by without staring. And this I did.

'What's that funny noise?' said Nigel one day, as we walked away from the couples, along a tree-lined path patterned in sunlight. 'Listen. It's a sort of ghostly flapping kind of noise.'

'It's up there,' said David.

And looking up into the overhanging branches I saw a large piece of light coloured material, fluttering as the wind tugged at its drooping corner.

'It's a bit of parachute. Can we get it down?' Nigel was already surveying the tree, looking for footholds.

'Do you think a German pilot came down?'

'More likely a parachute flare,' David said, authoritatively. 'Or it could've been a *land mine*,' he added, so I quickened my pace away from the overhanging branch.

We left the piece of flapping parachute and decided to explore the far side of the park instead. Away across the grass we could see two abandoned lorries, each in an advanced state of disrepair. They had been driven or pushed on to the edge of the grass and just left to disintegrate. Nigel ran over to them and climbed up into one of the empty cabs. I pulled myself up after him and sitting on the hard metal seat frames we pretended we were driving, while David inspected the remains of the rusting engines.

'They're dangerous,' said Mother, when she heard about the lorries. 'You mustn't go near them. And another thing, you must *never* pick up anything you see lying on the ground. It doesn't matter what it looks like. You might think it's just an ordinary pencil, but it could explode.'

'*Explode!*' we chorused.

Mother was adamant. But she had heard warnings on the wireless about anti-personnel devices being dropped. Some became known as 'butterfly bombs', because they floated to the ground like winged seeds. As many of them would be picked up, they were designed to look like familiar objects — but they exploded as soon as they were examined.

We heeded Mother's stern warning and picked nothing up. But sometimes we went to look at the abandoned lorries, to watch other children climbing over the damaged hulks; and sometimes, despite her warning, we climbed up too.

'Race you to the Swiss Cottage,' said Nigel, the next time we went to Singleton Park. And we chased across the wide expanse of grass.

'There's a queue,' I said, catching him up when he stopped by the path.

'There's always a queue.'

But we joined the long, winding line of children, for today was the day that the Swiss Cottage, flanked by trees in the centre of the park, became an infrequently opened café. While I shuffled along waiting for my turn, I looked at the sparse display of rock buns and cakes, wondering what I would buy. Cakes, as usual, were beyond my means.

'Can I have a roll, please?' I asked, timidly.

The Swiss Cottage, Singleton Park

The Educational Gardens

'A roll on the grass?' said the fat, leering man behind the counter; he made the same exhausted joke each time. At first I had giggled, but I soon learnt to ignore him.

Sometimes, when David was in charge of us, we stared through tall wrought-iron gates at a profusion of multicoloured plants in the Educational Garden. This was one of the fascinations of Singleton Park, but a large notice pronounced: 'No unaccompanied children under 12 years admitted'. It wasn't the plants we wanted to see, it was being allowed in that mattered.

'When I'm twelve I'll take you both in,' said David. But I knew we would have to wait another whole year.

'What a toff!' said my teacher, as I walked into the cloakroom proudly wearing my light blue matching coat and hat. I wasn't sure what a 'toff' was, but it didn't sound unkind.

I had been given the matching set for a special occasion when we lived in Swindon, and then it was saved for 'best'. But there were no 'best' occasions any more. So I wore it to school before it was out-grown, for now that clothing coupons had been introduced, only the most necessary clothes could be bought.

'It's a little on the large side,' Mother would say, when we occasionally bought something new. 'But you'll soon grow into it.'

Some clothes were patched and handed down, and shirt collars were reversed if a ragged white line appeared. To help preserve precious coupons Mother turned sheets sides-to-middle when the centre wore thin. And often our parents went without to prevent us from being squeezed into rapidly out-grown shoes and garments. But coupons and 'utility clothing' meant nothing to me — they were the concern of the Board of Trade.

The Ministry of Food's responsibility was to ensure the nation was adequately fed, so it encouraged local authorities to provide subsidised meals for schoolchildren, to make certain we were getting one balanced meal a day. Brynmill Infants' School hadn't heeded this encouragement, mainly because most children lived near enough to go home. But I had a much longer walk to school, so instead of going home at midday I took Marmite sandwiches in a square red tin, with Oxo printed in familiar white letters on each side.

The few of us who stayed were unsupervised, as we sat at our double desks with double seats attached. Each day when the teacher left the room she told us to behave; so we did. Then one lunchtime one of the boys clambered on to his desk and like sheep we all followed, laughing, shouting and stamping our feet as he was doing. Just as the teacher came to see the cause of the noise, the others climbed down and slid silently into their seats. Only I was left standing there.

'I put you on your *honour*,' the teacher said, looking at me in surprise. 'Having packed lunch is a *privilege*, you know.'

Bright red with shame I wanted to crawl away. I had never been reprimanded at school before and I felt like a criminal.

I knew Mother wasn't happy that I had to have sandwiches in the Infants', while David and Nigel could have a hot school meal each day, and somehow she arranged for me to go to the junior school for my lunch. So instead of joining the small sandwich group, I left my school with the home-going infants and climbed the hill to the 'big' school. Timidly I walked in past the tall iron gates, across the playground to push open the heavy door of the main hall. At once I was amidst a sea of faces; a clattering, chattering roar of noise and the clinging smell of cabbage, swede and hot gravy. I hated it.

Inside the hall I stood and looked for David amongst the rows of benches. When I spotted him, I squeezed past the backs of the 'big' children and sat up to the long trestle table in the space saved beside him. What David thought of this arrangement I didn't know, but he can't have liked his shy little, bespectacled sister invading his world.

Sometimes I arrived late, when everyone had been served and an over-full plate of steaming food was waiting for me. Sometimes I would have to pipe up in a small voice that I didn't want very much, or I would whisper to David and he would say it for me. Struggling through those meals and the smell of hot, unwelcome food was an agonising experience. Each time I climbed the hill and was confronted by that powerful smell, I had the same sinking feeling that stayed vividly with me, even after the arrangement ended.

But going to Brynmill had its compensations. The schools were close to the coast, and from the road we could see the light, bright sky that indicated the wide expanse of sea. Occasionally, on warm sunny days, our mother collected us from school and we ran down to the beach. While we ate our picnic, we sat on a narrow strip of sand to watch the waves curling and tumbling into the water.

On other days we saw the sea from the top of the old trams, that rattled their way along the Mumbles Railway. And once, with the brisk sea wind ruffling our hair and tugging at our clothes, we climbed the long gravelly path between Caswell and Langland Bays. At the top we looked out over the sea. But we could never go down to the water, because of the rolls of barbed wire that stretched along the beach, and other defences laid in case of invasion.

As summer crept into autumn and winter fast approached, news bulletins were reporting appalling, icy conditions on the Russian front, where the battle scene had shifted. Although this was of little interest to me, my parents were deeply concerned by the way the war was spreading.

Then came a devastating announcement. On the 7th December an estimated 150 Japanese bombers had attacked Pearl Harbour, the chief American Naval base in the Pacific. Several anchored ships were reported to have been hit, and two battleships, the *Oklahoma* and the *Arizona*, sunk.

With this unexpected escalation, the USA came into the conflict and the formal declaration of war against Japan was announced. The following day came tragic news of the sinking of HMS *Prince of Wales* and *Repulse* by Japanese bombers. Three days later we heard that Germany and Italy had declared war on the USA. Now the whole world seemed to be at war.

Japanese aircraft carriers started simultaneously attacking the chain of American Pacific Island bases, thousands of miles apart, as well as the British outposts of Hong Kong, Singapore and Malaya. Silently my parents realised that our over-stretched military forces would need to be stretched even further. But the fighting abroad still had little meaning for me. Only the immediate everyday happenings were part of my life. And I had the school Christmas party to look forward to.

Even so, talk of American war machinery, troops and airmen being seen throughout Britain filtered through to me; and we heard that Flying Fortresses and Liberators now flew from newly-constructed airfields.

'Does it mean the war will soon be over?' I asked.

'A little boy called David is coming to stay with us,' Mother announced one day. She told us that his mother drove an ambulance with Auntie Madge in South London. 'So little David needs a holiday.'

At almost three, 'Little David' seemed a quiet, unresponsive child

— even I could see that. When he was sitting in his cot, Nigel and I tried to play a game of 'peep bo' with him. We put a cot blanket over his head, expecting him to take it off, so that we could shout 'Bo'. Instead, Little David just sat there until we took it off again. After that we often covered him with a blanket to see how long he would stay there. It was a great game — until Mother stopped us.

Not long after Little David's stay with us came to an end, a large black pram appeared in the hall and I peeped inside to see the tiny baby. Mother looked after her during the day, while the baby's mother was on 'essential war work'. But babies were far too young for me to play with, so I quickly lost interest, particularly now the end of term was fast approaching.

On the day of the infants' Christmas party, we pushed and jostled into the school hall for games, and a wonderful tea of jellies, cakes and blancmanges. As soon as the empty plates had been cleared away, we were told to sit quietly on the hall floor for a surprise, because someone had come to see us. The twittering of small voices stopped abruptly when the head teacher announced:

'Here he is, children, *Father Christmas!* And he's got a present for each one of you.' Squeals of delight issued from the hall.

I nudged the girl next to me and whispered, 'He's not real.'

'He is you know,' she whispered back.

'He's not!'

'He *is!*'

I kept quiet after that, and one by one the infants around me went to collect a present. But I refused to go up for mine because I knew it was all pretence, and somehow I wanted everyone to know I didn't believe. Eventually, when I was the only child left without a present, I was persuaded to go to Father Christmas. I swaggered up condescendingly, grinning with what I thought was superior knowledge. No one understood my strange behaviour. But I remembered the previous Christmas and the forgotten stockings.

With Christmas over and the large black pram no longer standing in the hall, I heard that a small girl called Janet Bridge was coming to stay for a while. Now that sounds better, I thought.

4. Flying over the Trees: 1942-1943

I held tightly to my blankets while small, fair-haired Janet tugged at one corner. But the more I clung on — trying to pretend I was going to sleep — the more Janet tugged. Slowly, as I clutched less and less, they slid to the floor.

Janet and I had twin beds in the large front bedroom with the round bay window, and the first night she arrived the blanket-pulling had started. I soon realised that even though she was two years younger, Janet was a far more lively and forceful character than I was, and I had the cowardly thought that if I ignored her she would stop. Instead, my ordeal went on for several nights as Janet laughed her way through my discomfort.

Usually she pulled the blankets off completely, exposing my cold taut body, or the bed became such a muddle I had to get out to remake it. But her blanket-pulling finally infuriated me. The next night, before she had time to start, I dragged her blankets to the floor. There was peace after that and I learnt a valuable lesson. And I soon found that now I was no longer the youngest I could join in the teasing, instead of being the one to be teased.

I had started knitting squares with unravelled wool from old jerseys, and had just learnt to cast on, so one afternoon sitting at the dining room table, I cast on a few stitches for Janet. Laboriously, she worked her way through a row while I showed her what to do. I noticed the boys standing round watching, but as I was the one who could knit, I carried on showing Janet.

'Look,' said David, suddenly, and he bent down, pretending to pick up a small circle of wool he supposedly found on the floor. 'You've dropped a stitch!' As Janet tried to fit the 'stitch' into her knitting, we each found more stitches on the floor, until Janet became so cross she abandoned her knitting.

Some days Nigel and I dressed up in old clothes tucked away in the Underworld, waiting to go to factories for rags, cotton or wool. In shirts down to our knees, with waistcoats, scarves and incongruous hats, we introduced each other in turn to Janet. Janet, we soon realised, was convinced by our disguises. Even a small piece of black insulating tape as a moustache transformed us into strange new people.

I liked the Underworld. It was a treasure-house of useful things: the collections for re-cycling, pieces of unused furniture, empty sacks and all the other oddments waiting in case they were needed. In amongst them, by the earthenware sink, was a boiler and mangle for the steamy washing that on wet days draped from wall to wall. But for us, the contents of the Underworld had far more interesting uses.

When David was at choir practice one Sunday morning and Janet was with our mother, Nigel and I hurried down the narrow stairs to the Underworld, for Nigel had an idea. 'Get one of those deck chairs,' he said, pulling roughly at a plank of wood.

'There're some boxes . . .' I began, but Nigel interrupted.

'Hurry up or Janet'll be down.'

We dragged the deck chairs, planks of wood and old boxes into the garden, then arranged and rearranged them on the back lawn. Finally we were just enclosing our masterpiece in old sacks, when we heard Janet stomping down the narrow staircase.

'What are you doing?' she said, coming out to see where we were. She stared quizzically at the sack-covered shape.

'It's our plane,' said Nigel. 'We're going for a spin!'

'I want to come.'

'Well all right, but you've got to sit still. We're going right up in the sky! Get in this side.'

He pushed Janet through to the 'cockpit', leaving only a small aperture open, while I squeezed through to the back from the other side, and squatted down in the dark framework of deck chairs.

'Ready to go,' Nigel called, climbing into the cockpit beside Janet. And with suitable noises he pulled on the 'joystick' as the plane supposedly started to move. Crouching in the back under strong smelling sacks, I slipped my arm through the edge of a deck chair and picked up a branch of leaves, carefully hidden along the side under the sacking.

'Going up!' I heard Nigel say.

So I rustled the leaves past the cockpit for Janet to see.

'Just flying over the trees,' he said, as the leaves thrashed about, and he manoeuvred the plane with hair-raising twists and turns of the joystick. After his avoidance measures, we flew over houses and shops, roads and more trees, as Nigel relayed to us what he could see. 'Sit tight,' he shouted to Janet. 'You might fall out!'

With more waving of leaves, the plane started to land, bumpily, while I vigorously rattled the deck chairs.

'Hold on. We're skidding along the ground.' Nigel was prolonging the flight with maximum effect.

'I want to go again!' said Janet, her blue eyes shining. So up we went. Sometimes Nigel let me take the controls, while he waved the branch of leaves, and each time Janet thought she was sailing through the sky.

But while we were happily flying, the war was galloping on. The production of German U-boats had trebled, and in 'wolf packs' they hunted Allied convoys. In March and April, in an attempt to halt this vast increase, the wireless announced that the RAF had bombed Lubeck and Rostock, where U-boats were constructed. Iron-ore and other vital raw materials passed through these ports, too, and there were Heinkel aircraft works and shipbuilding yards at Rostock.

Between April and June Hitler ordered reprisal raids. He selected historic cities, marked by three stars in the Baedeker travel guides, and soon details of raids on Exeter, Bath, Norwich, York and Canterbury came through. They became known as the Baedeker Raids, and we learnt later that German radio reported: 'This Exeter is a jewel. We have destroyed it.'

While the harassing Baedeker Raids continued, we heard of the RAF's thousand-strong bomber attack on Cologne, a centre of rail communications and war industries. In June came a similar raid on Essen. Then followed night raids on industrial towns in the Ruhr valley, and daytime raids on strategic targets by American bombers. Results were devastating — but the war continued. Swansea also continued to be bombed, spasmodically, so Janet returned home.

I had thought that if I were kneeling by my bed saying my nightly prayers when a bomb landed, the small piece of ceiling above my head would stay intact. But when one night an air raid warning sounded, I didn't wait to find out. Abruptly, I finished my prayers and hurried down to the shelter with David and Nigel. Our parents didn't come down, but I knew Father was ill in bed with a high fever; I had peeped in to see him earlier when he was fast asleep. So while I listened to the threatening planes and bursts of shelling, punctuated by the sudden screech of bombs, I wondered what was happening.

Despite the build-up of ack-ack fire and enemy planes, Father felt too ill to get up. Mother pleaded with him to go downstairs where she would make up a bed on the settee. And finally he agreed. As she hurried away with blankets and pillows, he pulled himself from his bed and started shakily down the stairs. He had just started down when he heard a nearer thud than the thumps and crashes outside. It was followed by a sudden loud hammering on the front door, which burst open.

'Put that light out!' shouted an irate warden, and he dashed into the hall and clattered up the stairs.

Starting back up the stairs after the warden, Father saw choking fumes and smoke lit by a bright light coming from his bedroom. When he looked in through the haze, he realised, with horror, that the bed he had just left was on fire. Miraculously, all thoughts of illness vanished, as wardens and firefighters hurried in with sand and stirrup pumps. Down in the Underworld we heard their shouting voices and running feet.

When the smouldering mattress was finally extinguished, they found the remains of an incendiary bomb lodged in the spiral spring of the double bed. The metal spring had saved the incendiary from causing greater damage by containing it suspended over the floor — exactly below the spot where Father had been lying.

We stayed in the shelter all that night. But the next morning we

The Gower Road, Swansea

saw the gaping hole in our roof and the spilled tiles. David, Nigel and I went to the top of Eversley Road and down Gower Road, to see the pock-marked pavements where shrapnel and bomb casings had gouged their mark. And we saw people, picking up the threads of life and carrying on.

This time our own clearing-up began, as water had seeped everywhere: over the carpets, the furniture and through the ceiling. I hated the pungent smell of burning mattress that clung to the house for days. But we knew we had been lucky; other people's houses had been destroyed — and other people hadn't survived.

One early-summer morning I woke and felt a severe pain in the lower part of my right leg. As I tried to get out of bed, the pain grew more intense and it was difficult to walk. I developed a high temperature and could hardly bare even a sheet to rest on the leg. Father made a cradle to take the weight of the sheet and leave my leg free, and much consultation ensued.

'What have you been doing?' they all asked.

All I could think of was trying to stand on a tennis ball, with the ball under my instep. But, no, that was not the cause. As the pain and temperature increased, I heard talk of my going into hospital. An operation? To do what? I knew going into hospital was a serious matter, because even the words were spoken in a slightly lowered voice with some reverence. So I was pleased when no ambulance came for me. Instead, the doctor prescribed the new cure-all, M and B tablets, and rest.

'Can I have the gramophone?' I asked, as I sat awkwardly in bed with my painful leg. And I flattened a space on the sheet in readiness. Having the tiny wind-up gramophone was our greatest treat when we were ill.

David brought it in to me, with our three five-inch records. 'Don't lose these in the bed,' he said, handing me the wooden needles.

He helped me fix a needle into the slot, then left as I wound up the gramophone with its tiny handle. I alternated between 'Hand Me Down My Walking Cane' and the rhythmic 'Hawaiian War Chant', which we called 'Ah Way Ah Woyah' because that's what it sounded like. The third record I played sparingly. It was a treasured one-sided tin record Father had recorded for us when we lived in South London. Despite his inability to sing in tune, I loved hearing the distant crackle of 'Hello David, Nigel and Margaret', then the tinny sounds of 'Whose Afraid of the Big Bad Wolf'.

Gradually the excruciating pain in my leg eased and my temperature lowered. Periostitis was the pronounced verdict — inflammation around the bone shaft. But how or where I got the infection no one knew.

I was looking out of the sitting room window with Mother one morning, enjoying the cosy feeling of being better but not well enough to go to school, when the milkman's horse and cart drew up outside. We watched as neighbours came out of their houses carrying an assortment of jugs and bowls for their milk. The milkman climbed down to the step of the cart, then jumped down to the road. He picked up his measuring jug and dipped it into the churn to fill the first container. Between customers he put the jug down on the step while he chatted, then picking it up again he plunged it into the milk.

'Look at that!' said Mother, in horror. 'All those germs on the step are going straight into the milk churn.' We didn't know whether this was the cause of my infection, but from then on the dairy took more care.

It may have been because of my leg, or it may have been because of the distance we had to walk to school, that I was told we would be leaving Brynmill and starting new schools in the autumn term. But first we had to visit the schools our parents had selected in nearby Uplands, an adjacent suburb.

I liked Oakleigh House the moment Mother and I walked into the bright, colourful classroom. No high ceilings and big windows here; just an ordinary house converted to a small school by adding an art room to the back. And there was the tiniest square playground I had ever seen, with only just room for one class at a time to play there. Mrs Bartlett-Williams, the kindly effusive principal, gladly showed us round the school. As we walked into one class, I saw children of my age busily cutting out pieces of coloured sticky paper. They all stopped cutting to stare when Mrs Bartlett-Williams introduced my mother to Mrs Muxworthy, the form mistress, while I stood shyly by.

'Carry on working, children,' said Mrs Muxworthy, in a soothing voice. And the cutting quickly restarted.

I watched as one by one the cut-out shapes were proudly taken to Mrs Muxworthy's desk. With great care each piece was positioned on to outline pictures of 'children of other lands', then the finished pictures were pinned around the walls. We looked into the art room next, and other classes, but secretly I hoped I would do some cutting and sticking one day, for the bright colourful classroom was the one I liked best.

At home Father read out the school prospectus. 'Staff,' he said, impressively. 'The school staff has teachers of considerable experience, some of whom are college trained and certificated by the Board of Education. School fees,' he read on, 'are five guineas a term, which includes stationery, use of books and handwork materials for pupils under eight years of age.'

There was an addition charge of five shillings per term for those over eight, but as I was not quite eight at the start of that autumn term, no additional fee was needed.

Change of schools meant school uniform to buy with precious clothing coupons. David and Nigel were starting at Dumbarton, a boy's preparatory school in Uplands, so they needed new brown blazers and jerseys with a brown and yellow cap and tie. And my uniform which was minutely detailed in the school prospectus, including 'slippers for indoor wear', would need more sparse coupons.

Struggling into my crisp white blouse, navy tunic and striped tie, I felt particularly grown-up. But my over-large navy blazer, with the school badge emblazoned on the pocket, was my proudest possession. It wasn't just school uniform, it was *best* too.

The smell of boiled milk seeped through the school each morning just before 'mid-morning recreation time'. It was followed by two large white jugs — one steaming — being carried into the classroom with a tray of assorted cups. At the start of the term we had handed in our own cup and made our choice of hot or cold milk. But one morning, when too much milk had been boiled, someone had to have hot instead of cold. I slid down in my seat hoping it wouldn't be me, as I watched Mrs Muxworthy looking round the class.

'Margaret won't mind hot milk today will you Margaret?' she said, coaxingly. 'I know you can be a big girl.'

So I swallowed it down with great difficulty.

Each Saturday morning I was taken to a strange house near the school. Here, for an additional fee of £1 . 5s each term, I slowly worked my way through Adam Carse's 'Toyland Tunes', 'The

ABC Short Tutor' and 'An Alphabet of Exercises for the Pianoforte'. Once I got used to the strange house, I enjoyed my piano lessons and soon started to make excellent progress.

But reading was much harder. I liked the sound of Milly-Molly-Mandy and I enjoyed all the stories — provided they were read to me. I loved the Ameliaranne books, too, and my anguish was unsurpassed when Ameliaranne went to a party and tried to take food home in her large green umbrella, for her numerous brothers and sisters. But I wished I could read all the words.

Then one day I saw a thick book lying on the kitchen table. Nigel had borrowed it from the library at the top of Eversley Road. Idly I picked it up to examine the picture of a burning house on the cover. *The Mystery of the Burnt Cottage* by Enid Blyton it said, although I guessed some of the words. I flicked through the pages and saw that there were only a few pictures, even so I turned to the first page and started to read. And to my

I liked Milly-Molly-Mandy

surprise I found I didn't need a picture on every page; the story carried me along. Laboriously struggling with the words, guessing and missing many of them, I forged my way through, totally absorbed.

To me, the story happened in Swansea! I was there with Bets, Pip, Larry and Daisy. I saw and smelt the cottage burning down; I met with interest their new friend Fatty and his dog Buster. And I almost knew and was irritated by Mr Goon the bumbling policeman.

Suddenly, the world of books had opened — just a chink — beyond the reading books at school. I still needed simple language to encourage me to read, and I created my own mental image of the characters. But my first glimpse into *The Mystery of the Burnt Cottage* was a tremendous leap forward.

'Who can tell the time?' Mrs Muxworthy asked, as we finished our carefully drawn writing patterns one morning.

Quickly I put up my hand, then thrilled I had been chosen to go on an errand, I left the classroom and walked down the carpeted stairs to the hallway to find the clock. The big round face stared down at me from the wall and I looked up to see what the numbers said. But there were no numbers. Instead I saw strange Is, Vs and Xs. I peered at them, trying to work out what they meant, and wondered where the numbers should go.

I didn't want to go back to the classroom without working it out because I knew I could tell the time, so I went on standing there. If the big hand is pointing halfway down it would be quarter past, but it's not quite there so it's not quarter past, and the little hand's pointing straight up. . . At that moment another girl came to find me. Between us we worked out the time and went back proudly to tell Mrs Muxworthy.

In solemn voice, a few days later, Mrs Bartlett-Williams was telling us of the death of someone close to the school. We sat at our desks, staring silently, because she sounded so serious. 'And I would like you all to bring sixpence for a collection.'

Once out in the tiny playground several of us talked this over in similarly serious tones. Who had died? What would happen? Where was the body? Then one boy made a joke of it and gradually we all became giggly and over-excited. But not knowing the person who had died, we were unsure how to react.

By the time I reached home at lunch time, laughter had turned to tears and I cried and cried. I had never heard or talked about death before. Even dead cats or dogs, I was told, were 'sleeping'. That afternoon I was kept home from school so the subject could be forgotten. And when I returned the next day nothing more was said.

There were ice patterns on the windows now, as I buttoned myself into my 'liberty bodice' each morning and wriggled my legs into thick lisle stockings. And when I ran down the road for school, sliding my feet through crisp yellow leaves, my breath puffed white in the cold air.

Waving good-bye to Mother, I ran to catch the bus with a friend and her mother. I turned again, waved both hands to show my lovely blue and white striped gloves, then ran on, tripped, slipped and skidded along the pavement on knees and hands. Picking myself up — and my glasses which had miraculously stayed intact — I looked down at the jagged holes that had appeared in my lisle stockings; and then at the missing palms in my gloves. The blood and grit didn't worry me, only the sight of those holes in my new gloves. My mother wouldn't be cross, I knew that, but I was sad because she had only just finished knitting them.

I carried on to school and it was this day, of all days, that I was chosen to mind the nursery class during their afternoon rest. Apprehensively I sidled into the adjoining darkened classroom, where thin palliasses were laid across the floor. I noticed a small mound of blanket on each one, and as I stood nervously watching, the small mounds started to wriggle and whisper. Whispering turned to chattering and giggling, then someone noticed the jagged holes in my thick stockings.

'Look, there's blood!'

'Why've you got holes in your stockings?'

One by one small children rolled off their beds to have a closer look at my knees, until they were all milling round me. I tried to quieten them so that Mrs Muxworthy wouldn't hear; I tried to hustle them back to rest, but I was out of my depth. Thankfully the connecting door opened and Mrs Muxworthy came to put someone else in charge. I was never asked again.

Fortunately, during that winter term at Oakleigh House there were no more air raids. It was another town's turn. Declining raids after the three-night blitz had been followed by a long lull, which extended beyond Christmas and into February.

'Mrs Evans is coming to look after you all this evening,' Mother announced, one bright February day. 'Daddy and I are going to a dinner-dance.'

I had heard them talking about the 16th being the BHS dinner-dance. And with rising Allied victories and only one raid on Swansea seven months earlier, they decided it would be safe to go out for the first evening for many months — possibly even years. So when Mrs Evans arrived we waved them good-bye, as they set off through the blackout to the dinner-dance near the docks.

The evening was in full swing when the band stopped abruptly. To everyone's surprise the MC announced that an air raid warning had sounded and there was now a 'red alert'.

Mother's one thought was to get home so we would all be together, and by the time they had made their way out into the street, they were thrust into a night bright with flares, criss-crossed in search lights, with sounds of pounding guns and throb of enemy planes. They ran from the building, down a side street and along another, weaving their way through the empty roads.

Above the noise of gunfire and the roaring, crashing of bombs, rose the sudden screech of a plane. It sounded to be diving straight towards them, machine gunning the road as it zoomed down. Throwing themselves under a parked vehicle, the only immediate cover, they heard the splatter, splatter of bullets whipping past them. Then the plane was gone; its sound lost in the terrifying clutter of noise. Crawling back out again, they hurried on and saw a solitary man coming down the road towards them.

'You all right?' he called, as they neared him.

'Yes, thanks. We sheltered under that lorry.' And they indicated the lorry behind them.

'Blimey!' said the man. 'I just left that. It's full of petrol!'

Shaken, they carried on with their dash for home and found us safely sheltering in the Underworld. The following morning our own road was cordoned off because of an unexploded bomb.

Two years in Swansea had slipped slowly by with much to get used: two different schools, air raids, and sometimes the Welsh language to confuse us. But there were always wonderful sounding names to conjure with — Fforest-fach, Tre-boeth, Bon-y-maen, Cwmdonkin — and I like the sound of Oystermouth and Black Pill.

With diminishing raids, my simple daily happenings had become more important to me, as I settled into each new routine. I learnt to skip and played dolls with my new friend, Margaret Roberts, who lived opposite us. Father took me to Mr Tooth, the dentist, and afterwards bought me a penny currant bun. And from time to time I visited Mrs Evans next door.

Once Mrs Evans gave me a beautiful Camberwell Beauty butterfly displayed in a metal case, and I was even more delighted when she gave me a small polished box containing forty-five tiny blocks of different samples of wood. Each one was numbered and listed and varied in colour from the palest cream through to shiny black.

And we had singing round the piano — magical times when we almost forgot the war — when Mother played all our old favourites from our sing-songs in the shelter.

Despite the slogan 'Is your journey really necessary?' and after much deliberation, Father made arrangements for Mother to take we three children by train to Beckenham in Kent, to visit Grandpa for his sixty-fourth birthday. But we had no idea of what lay in store, and that this would be the end of our stay in Swansea.

5. They're Only Practising: Beckenham 1943

On Saturday 24th April, dressed in my school uniform for 'best', I climbed into a waiting train at Swansea Station with David, Nigel and our mother. We waved good-bye to Father as the train chugged away and we set off, back towards Swindon, on the all-day journey to Paddington.

I was looking forward to seeing Grandpa, my mother's father. To me he was a tall, rough cheeked, rugged sort of man, and I thought he could do *anything* because I was told he had once manoeuvred a piano down the stairs on his own.

As I squeezed into the corner of the crowded carriage, I remembered my visits to see him before the war, when he joked and teased in a grandfatherly way. We played in his garden and stood by the rockery for a rarely-taken photograph. And he bounced me on his knee and called me Crystal Palace face because of my little round glasses. Once the war started, his visits to us had been infrequent, but I remembered his stories about 'the Great War'.

Years later, Mother told us about Grandpa and how he had been in the 7th City of London Regiment during the first world war. Afterwards he had become a 'Territorial', so being a staunch military man he was disappointed in 1939 when he was not able to rejoin the army. Mother said she thought the reason was not so much his age, but because he had a German housekeeper.

Hella had applied to be Grandpa's housekeeper several years before the outbreak of war, but she wanted to return to her 'beautiful mountains' for three months each year. Although Grandpa hadn't agreed to allow her three months' leave, Hella did return home for shorter holidays. Whenever she had any other spare time she travelled around England sketching and painting, and these paintings she took back to Bavaria on her trips home.

On one occasion, when Hella was unable to return home, she

insisted on photographing Grandpa standing by her easel. The easel displayed her latest painting, so instead of taking the painting back she sent the photograph that showed it.

When Mother was telling us the story, she said she thought Hella's paintings had concealed maps of strategic military installations, which Hella dutifully handed over to the German military authorities on her visits home. Whether this was true, or whether it was even possible, we didn't know. But as soon as war started Hella was interned in Holloway Prison, where she stayed for the duration of the war. One thing was certain: Grandpa — the most patriotic of Englishmen — would have been devastated had he known he was unwittingly involved in any sort of deception.

But I knew nothing of all this on that Saturday morning as the train steamed away from Swansea. We expected it to stop at every station and that we might be shunted off the main line to let more vital trains go through — we had heard of these possibilities before we set out. Even so, the journey seemed endless.

As the hissing, clanking engine slowed to a stop at each station there was no way of knowing where we were, because the names had been removed when invasion had seemed imminent. So while we watched the changing scenery, ate home-made sandwiches at intervals through the day, or played I-Spy, quietly so we wouldn't disturb the other passengers, the journey dragged on.

When we approached a tunnel a dim blue light came on in the centre of the gloomy carriage. A soldier stood up and quickly raised his door window with its long leather strap. It had been opened a few notches, but now bitter-tasting smoke trapped in the tunnel had drifted in. He pulled down the door blinds, too, but soon the train emerged back into the afternoon, the dim blue light went out and he raised the blinds.

Eventually, exhausted after our day of travelling, we reached Paddington. And there, waiting by the barrier to meet us, was Grandpa. We ran over to him and he hugged and kissed us, as laughing and chattering we told him about the journey. For a brief moment the war seemed far away.

From Paddington we caught a bus across bomb-torn London to Victoria, where we clambered into a train to Kent House Station in Beckenham. From here we set off on the mile or so walk to Queen's Road. I was tired after the long journey and struggled with the walk, but the excitement carried me on. Grandpa insisted

We stood by the rockery

*We climbed
inside the
hammock*

*Grandpa's
house*

on carrying our big leather suitcase on his head. He said he was used to carrying loads in this way at Smithfield meat market, so our case was easy. And to my delight he wore my school beret to ease the pressure.

Miss Garvie, the Scottish housekeeper who had replaced Hella, was at the house to meet us, busy in the kitchen preparing a welcome cup of tea. I looked up at the tall straight-backed figure, with her glasses and greying hair, but it was her deafness that intrigued me most. I had been told to speak loudly and to mouth my words, but Miss Garvie mostly misunderstood my quiet mumblings.

Grandpa talked enthusiastically about his new Morrison shelter, which he was anxious to show us, so after our cup of tea Mother, Nigel and I followed him into the sitting room. The shelter, jutting out from the corner, took up a large part of the room, but it looked just like a large metal table to me. A dark maroon, tasselled cloth covered the top and hung down partly covering the cage-like sides.

Nigel and I peered inside, while Grandpa sat on the hard edge explaining the advantages of the cast iron table top, with its sturdy iron corners and wire-mesh clip-on sides. At the same time he reassured us of how safe and cosy we would be lying on the four-foot mattress, if we had to use it.

'It's as safe as houses,' he said, laughing and patting the metal surface. Then he fell back across the table top and lay still.

We joined in laughing, thinking he was playing one of his many jokes. But he remained still, and our laughter died with him. Hurriedly Nigel went to find Miss Garvie, while my distraught mother hustled me from the room.

I went upstairs out of the way, and David and Nigel soon joined me. We heard Auntie Flo arrive; other people came and went. Then Miss Garvie served supper for us in the kitchen, although I noticed the grown-ups didn't eat at all.

But I was confused. Where was Grandpa? Had he really *died*? I didn't appreciate the shock Mother must have had; the strain of the long train journey with three young children; the joy of seeing her father shattered by this sudden tragedy.

When my late bedtime came, I was surprised that I would have to share a double bed with Auntie Flo. But I was even more surprised when I found she had slipped the double under-pillow down the centre between us. I undressed in the unfamiliar room, folding my clothes neatly because Auntie Flo would be there later. Then, with the light switched off, I knelt up to the big bed and prayed hard.

I determined to pray the same prayer for three nights: 'God bless Mummy, Daddy, David, Nigel and Margaret, and please let Grandpa come alive again.' After all, I reasoned, the Bible said, 'And on the third day He rose again from the dead'. Surely it would work for Grandpa now?

Then I climbed in between the sheets and lay to one side, waiting for Auntie Flo to creep silently into the darkened room and lie on the other side of the bolster. Through the night I listened to her quiet breathing and heard the grandfather clock on the bend of the stairs, chiming its regular quarters.

The next morning David, Nigel and I were whisked away to Wallington in Surrey, to stay with Uncle Basil, Auntie Ethel and cousins Robert and Gill. No one mentioned Grandpa — at least not to me. But I continued to pray the same prayer; perhaps three nights wasn't long enough.

I was slightly awed by Uncle Basil, the second of Father's two elder brothers. Unlike his willowy sisters and tall brothers, Uncle Basil was short and wiry. He seemed aloof, and I felt I had to make a special effort to be 'grown-up' when he was there, although he was always kind to me. But on one occasion, when he explained the intricacies of the doll's house he had made, we were almost on equal terms.

The doll's house fascinated me. It was an exact replica of his own house — a converted stable — with the front door at the back. From behind a high wall on one side of the beautiful garden came mouth-watering smells from a chocolate factory, while along the other side trickled the River Wandle. The doll's house presented the rear view with its dark oak front door, and opened out to show a magnificent staircase and galleried landing leading to the bedrooms. Every detail, even the furniture and lighting, had been faithfully reproduced.

Auntie Ethel, my Godmother, was the exact opposite of her quick, inventive, precise husband. Auntie Ethel was a kind, gentle dumpling, with a soft smile that was never far away. She was always the same, so we all responded to her quiet gentleness.

Only Robert and Gill were at home during our short stay. Jean, their elder sister, was away manning guns on the South Coast with the ATS, which I soon learnt meant Auxiliary Territorial Service. Robert had just started work, so he was out in the daytime, but Gill was full of fun, and being barely a year older than Nigel, we all played well together.

Chattering over its stony bed, the River Wandle was our favourite place to play. We floated logs down it, climbed on overhanging branches sheltering the bank, waded across the shallow bubbling water and dammed up the little streams that seemed to escape along the edges. I was so absorbed that time drifted by, and gradually I accepted that people can't come alive again — not even my Grandpa.

When we returned to Beckenham we were told we would not be going back to Swansea. David had passed the entrance exam to Alleyn's School in Dulwich, while he had been at Glenshee House, so our parents were anxious for him to start as soon as he could. And now, with fewer air raids, they felt it would be safe to look for a house in South London. Besides, we had lived through the blitz on Swansea so what else could be worse?

I thought of Oakleigh House and my friend Margaret Roberts in Eversley Road, and I wondered about another new school and another new house, but I was used to moving by now.

There was an air of optimism around as my parents discussed the Eighth Army's long-fought campaign in North Africa, which finally ended in May. In May, too, came the amazing news that the Mohne and Eder dams had been breached by RAF precision bombing. Millions of tons of water had cascaded through the Ruhr valley, destroying war factories, power stations, villages and railways in its path. And in July, RAF and American bombers attacked Hamburg one of the chief German U-boat bases.

The feeling of optimism was strengthened, when newspapers reported that Papua New Guinea had been regained from the Japanese by American and Australian troops. News also came through that the Russians were pushing back German forces on all fronts. At home, although no details were given, plans were forging ahead for a Normandy landing. Hope was in the air; the Allies were gaining ground; surely the end of the war could not be too far away?

Father returned to Swansea to pack up our belongings and

arrange our affairs. Then we settled down temporarily in Beckenham until Grandpa's house could be sold. The proceeds of the sale were to be divided equally between Mother and her younger sister, Gladys.

Auntie Gladys, my favourite of all our aunts, was outwardly solid, placid and dependable, yet bubbling below the surface lurked a fiery spirit and sense of humour so like Grandpa's. I knew Auntie Gladys was unmarried and worked with mentally-handicapped children, because she talked about the children in her care. And she said we three children were far harder to look after than they were, but then we took advantage of her kindness.

David started at Alleyn's straight away, travelling by train to West Dulwich station, then walking about a mile and a half through Dulwich Village and up Calton Avenue to the school. A private tutor in Latin, English and Maths, called Mr Judge, came to teach Nigel until he could start at Alleyn's in September. Meanwhile I enjoyed my freedom.

I didn't realise that girls weren't expected to need the same education as boys. I just knew I had more time to play. But having lost so much schooling through illness and moving, I was far behind in basic subjects. Reading was particularly difficult. Each school I went to seemed to have books with different words which I couldn't understand. I often wished I could read as well as Nigel, but I knew he had learnt at Glenshee House.

When I failed the entrance exam to James Allen Girls' School, the sister school to Alleyn's, everyone was kind and understanding. Coming from my gentle Oakleigh House, I was overawed by the whole experience. I sat, pondering the maths questions, not realising there was a time limit.

'Dears.' said Auntie Madge, in her typically expressive way. 'I'm *so* glad Margaret didn't pass the entrance examination. . .' She went on to say that she knew an excellent school for me at nearby Tulse Hill, where her friend, Miss Orme, was teaching.

So Mother and I went by bus from Herne Hill to visit St Martin-in-the-Fields High School for Girls. As we walked up Tulse Hill I could see the school notice board ahead of us, standing out in front of what looked like a large white-fronted, three-storey house. Behind it, as though falling away down the hill, stretched a massive four-storey extension. We walked in through a wide gateway and I looked down beyond the building to netball and tennis courts and a small field fenced off from the surrounding gardens.

This time I knew what to expect when I worked my way through the entrance exam. And this time I passed, ready to start at St Martin's the following September. But before then there would be more school uniform to buy: brown square-necked gym-slip, fawn square-necked blouse, a brown beret and another new blazer.

Until I started back at school, I was happy to play in the garden or swing in Grandpa's strong canvas hammock. I liked the hammock and remembered before the war climbing inside with David and Nigel, when Grandpa had taken a photograph of us. Now I pulled the sides up around me, gently drifting from side to side and watching the leaves rustling against the sky.

As soon as Mr Judge had left after his morning's tutoring, Nigel escaped into the garden. I climbed out of the hammock when I saw him looking inside the small garden shed one day. 'What are you looking for?' I asked, and looked in too.

There was little to play with, just Grandpa's gardening tools, hose pipe and other odds and ends neatly stacked against one wall, with several deck chairs leaning against each other on another wall. Nigel was pulling at one of the deck chairs, so I helped him drag them all out and prop them together on the back lawn.

Miss Garvie, who was staying on until the house was sold, came to see what we were doing. 'I'm glad to see you're tidying the shed,' she said, in her rich Scottish accent.

We were getting used to her accent, but her deafness made it difficult to explain that we were really building an aeroplane. So Miss Garvie left us while we flew through the sky in another flight of fantasy. But after soaring to dizzy heights we put back the deck chairs, neatly as she had pointedly hinted.

'I've got an idea,' said Nigel. 'Let's take turns crawling across the kitchen floor, without Miss Garvie seeing us. She won't hear us, so we've got to see how far we can get.'

I thought this sounded a great game, until Nigel added that the idea was to get so close that we could look up Miss Garvie's long skirt and see her pink knee-length knickers! We waited until Miss Garvie was in the kitchen, then peered round the door to make sure her back was towards us. Nigel said I was to go first, so I started to crawl, silently and stealthily across the stone-flagged floor. Behind me, half-hidden in the doorway, Nigel made sure I obeyed the rules and gave warning of Miss Garvie's possible moves.

I had just reached the centre of the floor when Miss Garvie turned round and saw me in mid-crawl. 'What're y'looking for, Margaret?'

'She's lost something,' shouted Nigel, quickly. And then to me, 'Have you found it yet?' So I pretended to pick up something from the floor and hurried out of the room.

The next day it was Nigel's turn, but having successfully crawled across the floor without being seen, Miss Garvie suddenly noticed him crouching down by her feet and hastily shoed us both from the kitchen.

Air raid warnings continued to come and go spasmodically, but I was used to the ritual of air raids by now. One night when the siren started wailing, we all trooped down to the sitting room as usual, and crawled into Grandpa's Morrison shelter — all, that is, except Miss Garvie. Mother ran upstairs and found her fast asleep in bed. But she refused to get up, and with no sound of an imminent raid Mother left her.

No sooner had she returned to the shelter than we heard the distant hollow boom of anti-aircraft guns. The increasing drone of German planes quickly followed, and behind it more ominous sounds were gathering. We lay in the shelter listening to the familiar start of a raid; the whining of falling bombs, the crunch of explosions. Miss Garvie still hadn't come down, so Mother dashed upstairs to get her.

By the time she reached the bedroom and had shaken Miss Garvie awake, the raid was in full spate. Guns blasting; planes throbbing; windows rattling. Above the noise Mother shouted to her to go down to the shelter. But Miss Garvie looked up sleepily and said in her broad Scottish accent, 'Och, go back to bed, Lily, they're only practising!'

After Father had returned from Swansea, we started house-hunting. It took time looking for somewhere within easy travelling distance of Alleyn's and St Martin's, but I enjoyed going round from house to house seeing the possible — and impossible — places to live. Few people were buying houses in London, so prices were low. Many houses had been abandoned at the beginning of the war, with little hope of selling them. Some were damaged by fire and water; all had overgrown gardens.

And then we found a house in Dulwich.

6. The House on the Corner: Dulwich 1943-1944

I fell in love with 107 the moment I saw it standing there on the corner of Burbage Road and Turney Road, half hidden behind a straggly laurel hedge. The triangular garden surrounding it was completely overgrown and had that curious smell of sun-warmed vegetation.

'Look, there's a swing,' I said, seeing the wooden frame rising above the waist-high grass. But the others were going indoors, so I followed them into the empty, musty house, stamping my echoing feet through unaccustomed space and up the stairs.

Our visit was brief, for we had a train to catch back to Beckenham, so we hurried up Burbage Road, past an ornamental drinking fountain into Gallery Road. I barely noticed Dulwich Picture Gallery as we hurried on past playing fields to West Dulwich station. I was thinking of the house we had just seen, and hoping we would soon be living there.

It wasn't just the house I liked, it was the 'village' too. Sturdy chestnut trees shading the wide village street, Dulwich Park and the many tree-lined sports' fields made a lush, leafy oasis, and gave a secluded country feeling. It didn't seem like London.

The owners were delighted, if not surprised, to find a buyer in wartime, so a reasonable price was agreed. Even so, there would be ground rent to pay to Dulwich College Estates and upkeep far greater than on our previous rented houses. But I had no idea about any potential money worries. All that concerned me was moving to South London, to a house I wanted to live in the moment I saw it.

Before the move I was allowed to choose between the front and back single bedrooms. 'I'll have the front one,' I said, at once. 'It's got a bell push.'

The bell push, connecting to a display of service bells above the kitchen door, was a relic of former times, David told me. But I wasn't really interested in service bells and I didn't mention my main reason for wanting the room — it was at the head of the stairs where I could more easily run down to the shelter, when an air raid warning sounded.

Had I chosen the room at the back, beyond two airing cupboards, I thought I might be forgotten. It seemed a long way from the small, square landing, but Nigel liked this room and the slightly cut-off feeling it had. The only other single bedroom, we called the boxroom, would be useful when friends and relations stayed. David was given the front bay-windowed, double bedroom, because our parents preferred the double room at the back of the house, overlooking the garden.

Looking out of their bedroom window, over the fence and past an elderly oak, I saw a playing field stretching away to a railway embankment on the far side. And halfway across the field, above a low wooden pavilion, hung what looked to me like a massive legless elephant surveying the land.

'Bernard' the barrage balloon, as we immediately called it, was there to protect us, and I soon learned that it was part of the defence system around London. A taut cable, to deter bombers, kept Bernard gently swaying, and we heard a constant hum as the cable vibrated and sang in even the slightest breeze. At first I thought the bulky body was for 'catching' German planes by enveloping them, and looking up at the huge silver balloon I wondered what would happen if a plane crashed into Bernard.

On the day we moved, David stayed to help while Nigel and I were packed off to play with Stuart Macpherson. Stuart was three months older than Nigel, and our mothers had met before the war, pram-pushing in nearby Ruskin Park. Although Stuart now lived some distance away, up at the top of Herne Hill, I didn't mind missing the move because he was always kind to me and never argued like Nigel did. And 'Mrs Mac' spoilt me unashamedly.

As soon as we were collected from Stuart's house, and had made the long return walk, back down Red Post Hill and through Dulwich Village, Nigel and I bounded up the stairs to see our new rooms. I stood in my doorway surveying the large solid wardrobe, with a full-length mirror on the door, and an equally large dressing table with its own tilting mirror. I had never had a matching bedroom suite before, but I remembered seeing the furniture in Grandpa's house.

Between the bed and the outside wall, a narrow upright bookcase showed its bare shelves, while just inside the doorway a cardboard box was waiting to be unpacked. As I delved into the box, the old grandfather clock downstairs chimed a sudden reminder of Grandpa. No one had spoken about Grandpa's death, so silently I learnt to accept it. His clock now stood in the hall as though it had always been there, with its regular ticking and slight whirring before it chimed the quarter-hours.

It was a friendly sort of sound, I thought, and half listening to the comforting clock I unpacked my Camberwell Beauty butterfly and the polished box of wood samples from Swansea. I displayed them on a narrow mantelshelf above a tiny, temporarily blocked-in fireplace, then I started to arrange and rearrange my books. In their rooms, I could hear David and Nigel busily sorting out too.

With toys and books in place, I ran downstairs to investigate, glancing briefly into the bay-windowed room at the front of the house. We called it the dining room, because it contained Grandpa's massive carved sideboard and our own table and chairs. But on either side of the brick fireplace I saw Grandpa's heavy black armchairs, with a fine red dragon pattern crawling over them, and I knew my parents would sit here, listening to the frequent news bulletins on the brown, Bakelite wireless.

The room I really wanted to see — our own playroom — was at the back of the house. As I peeped round the door, there, protruding into the room stood the Morrison shelter, and Grandpa's words came flooding back: 'You'll be as safe as houses'.

We called it the dining room

Taking up part of one wall hung a large map of the world that had travelled with us wherever we went. I had seen my parents recording the day-to-day, step-by-step progress of the war on this map, but it meant little to me. I skirted round Grandpa's polished kitchen table in the centre of the room, past the old upright piano from Swansea and a comfortably-battered winged armchair, and made for the door that led to the garden.

Stepping on to a concrete path along the back of the house, I breathed in a warm, biscuity-smell from the long, spiky grass. As I stood there, surveying the wilderness, I felt a soft breeze blowing through strands of hair that had escaped the two small bunches I was trying to grow. Then seeing the wooden-framed swing, I started cutting my way through with a pair of nail scissors!

I needn't have worried, for our parents were keen gardeners and soon we were all helping to clear the weeds and long grass. The more we helped, the more paths we uncovered, so David, Nigel and I named each one. The less overgrown front garden was easy. We called the path leading up to the front door, 'Oxford Street', while 'Cert Street' led from the the garage to the gate. And so, quite simply, the front garden became the start of our imaginary world. We called it Devizes.

'Devizes' had been germinating in our minds ever since we stood in the unmade garden in Swindon, wishing we could make our own real town. We had often heard the intriguing name, but now, here in this wonderful overgrown garden, we had the perfect setting. And gradually we created more names for the 'roads' and their resident families.

'We'll call the back garden Brookley,' said Nigel, liking the sound of the name. 'And this is Hencher Road where the Butterfields live.' He indicated a newly-cut path from the back of the garage up to the fruit trees. As soon as we came across the fruit trees — in Devizes Hill — we picked and ate the unexpected apples, pears and plums, while Mother made jam and bottled the surplus fruit in kilner jars for the winter.

We uncovered 'Meadows Reach', the little path behind the bird bath on the edge of 'The Meadow' (the weed-covered lawn); 'Tivoli Gardens' and bizarre-sounding 'Mildew Crescent'. And when our parents started building a long, low rockery, 'Warsaw Road' appeared — we had heard the name on news bulletins on the wireless. Soon a smaller path climbed over the rockery, linking

'Warsaw Road' with long, winding 'Portsmouth Avenue'.

'That's Warport Avenue,' said David, and I could almost see the houses nestling on the hill: bare rockery stones, like huge boulders, indicating each one.

'Look, I've found a dead bird,' I said to Nigel, when we were 'council workers' with our wartime heavy rescue lorries, which looked remarkably like old galvanised buckets to anyone who didn't know. I was taking earth to the new rockery and stooped down to touch the limp body. It was perfectly formed and looked as though it really was 'sleeping'.

'I'll bury it in Devizes Cemetery, then,' said Nigel.

'Where's that?'

'Here.' And he simply scraped away at the bare earth under the sumach bushes at the end of Portsmouth Avenue.

'Did you know "Mrs Blue's" just had a baby?' I announced, as soon as the funeral service was over.

'She must have had it in Brookley Cottage Hospital,' Nigel said, more intent on placing a small wooden cross on the bird's grave.

'Now the father must do what he has to do,' I added, knowingly.

Nigel straightened up, laughing. 'It's not done *afterwards*. It's done beforehand!'

'But if it's done first,' I argued, 'why does the mother say "I think I'm going to have a baby", when she would *know* she was going to have one?'

Standing under the sumachs by 'Devizes Cemetery', Nigel patiently explained the full facts of life as he knew them. He used our own familiar jargon, 'long things and short things', so it was easy to understand. The act — which I had no idea about — he called a 'do', and thereafter 'How do you do?' took on a whole new meaning. At school I repeated my amazing knowledge to my new friends, Mary Marsh and Gloria Gorringe, for by now I had already started at St Martin-in-the-Fields on Tulse Hill.

Being too busy with my own preoccupations to let the world outside impinge, it meant nothing to me that earlier in the year the Allies had liberated Sicily, then moved on into southern Italy to overthrow Mussolini; or that Italy had changed allegiance, even though Germany still had a stronghold in the north. It would have surprised me to have been told that fighting was on so many different fronts.

'War' meant one side lined up against another in fixed positions, not several armies fighting several countries throughout the world. So when rain beat a rhythm against the windows, I sat up to the playroom table with Nigel's lead soldiers and drew pictures of a whole army ready for battle. I made the front row of soldiers lie flat with rifles extended, the next row knelt on one knee, with rifles resting on raised knees, and the final row stood.

Having coloured the uniforms with red crayons, I went to find the others to show them my picture. I found them in the kitchen discussing the aunts latest project.

I had heard talk that Glenshee House School had closed; something to do with the Dutch and Danish boarders returning home at the start of the war and other children being evacuated. There was also talk of the aunts opening a bookshop, now that the school's fittings and furnishings had mostly been dispersed.

'Auntie Madge suggested that if you three go along to the school on Saturday, you can choose something from the odds and ends that are left over,' Mother was saying.

'What sort of things?' said David.

'You'd better go and see.'

On Saturday morning, we walked through Dulwich Village and along Village Way to Half Moon Lane and the old school.

'I bet there's not much left.' Nigel was ahead of us, pushing past rough bushes in the now sadly neglected garden.

We went round to the back of the empty building, where the doors in the floor-to-ceiling glass bay were wide open. But we hesitated in the doorway.

'*Dears!*' came an unusually high-pitched voice, and I saw Auntie Madge kneeling on the floor amongst a motley collection of bric-à-brac.

'Liberty Hall, dears,' whispered Nigel, imitating her normal voice. 'Come along inside!'

I stifled a giggle as I imagined the aunts, clasping their hands to their chests before their familiar greeting.

'Liberty Hall, dears,' said Auntie Madge, predictably. 'Come along inside!' We went into the large echoey room, as Auntie Madge rose to her feet, adding, 'Now, dears, you may choose two items each.'

With great delight I looked at the Aladdin's cave: at pictures leaning against bare walls, battered items of sports' equipment huddled together with vases, odd rusty gardening tools and other relics of the school's former glory. I examined them all, one-by-one. Finally I decided on my two items.

'This is first,' I said, indicating a small glass fronted display case with twelve individual tin containers for butterflies. 'And these are my second,' I added, after more deliberation. And I unearthed a set of limp-covered green hymn books.

'Whatever do you want those for?' said David, dismissively.

'Devizes,' I said, with triumph.

As we were leaving, Auntie Madge picked up a small polished board from the pile of oddments. 'This goes with the hymn books, Margaret dear.' And she handed me the hymn board with numbers displayed on the front.

When we arrived home I propped the hymn board on the piano, gathered up several chairs and arranged them in rows across the playroom. Then I carefully sat toy animals on the seats, and gave each one a limp green hymn book.

'I'm going to have a service,' I told Nigel.

So Nigel, wearing one of Father's white detachable collars back to front, solemnly officiated. 'There is a green hill far away,' we sang, dolefully. But we finished with a rousing chorus of 'Onward Christian Soldiers'.

We had concerts, cabarets and boxing matches in the playroom, too. The boys had two pairs of boxing gloves, and we used the old domed clock on the mantelpiece to start and stop the rounds.

'Listen, it makes a ting when you move the hands past twelve,' Nigel demonstrated. And this gave an authentic touch to our bouts.

But one evening, when Stuart was with us and I neglected to parry his left hook, my nose received the full force. Nigel and Stuart rushed me to the kitchen.

'I didn't *mean* to hit you,' said poor Stuart, grabbing a tea towel to mop up blood, streaming from my nose.

'You should've ducked,' said Nigel.

'What ever's happened?' Mother, hearing the commotion, hurried in to investigate.

'It's all right,' Nigel assured her, as she calmly took over, 'it's all part of Devizes.' Because *we* knew that Stuart was really Farmer Billson, who had suddenly become an accomplished boxer.

Having settled to yet another way of life, I was gradually getting used to St Martin's unfamiliar world, with a more formal approach to learning. Unlike Oakleigh House in Swansea, where Mrs Muxworthy taught every lesson, subjects here were taken by different members of the 'Preparatory Department', always referred to as mistresses not teachers.

'How many legs has a chicken?' asked Miss Orme, Auntie Madge's short prim friend, who took us for nature study.

Hands shot in the air, so I put mine up, too.

'Yes, Margaret?'

I stood up. 'Four,' I said, without conviction.

Sitting down again, I was consumed with embarrassment when, in front of the whole class, Miss Orme said in her quiet way, 'I suggest you look at your aunts' chickens, Margaret.'

By now, Grandma and the aunts had moved to a house in Calton Avenue, near Alleyn's School, and on our occasional visits we noticed a strong, sickly smell like rotting cabbage, pervading the old Victorian house. The smell seeped from a concoction bubbling on the kitchen stove and was even worse than the rare occasions when cod's heads were boiled up for the cat. But it indicated that Auntie Madge was about to feed the chickens.

Sometimes I wandered down the garden to watch them scratching around in their wire netting enclosure, and occasionally when Auntie Madge came with me she gave me one or two precious eggs to take home. I carried the eggs carefully up the garden while Auntie Madge, in her high-pitched calling-voice, encouraged the chickens to come for their 'mash'.

'Bathsheba, Bathsheba,' I could hear, as I went indoors to say good-bye to Grandma.

'Fancy calling a chicken *Bathsheba,*' I said to Nigel, when I reached home. And to my amazement I learned that the aunts had given each chicken a biblical name.

I liked their outrageously spoilt, long-haired tabby called *Barsophe*, which I spelt bar-so-fee, because that's how they pronounced it, but I was surprised that Barsophe was allowed to walk over the table and accept tit-bits at meal times. She generally ruled the house, which we felt was a surprising lapse on the part of our 'correct' aunts and matriarchal Grandma.

Our own cat, Tigger, David had originally found hiding under the laurel bushes in the garden. He noticed the beautiful grey tabby, with her perfectly symmetrical black, grey and white roundel on each side, and coaxed her out with a saucer of milk.

'I expect she's bombed out. . .'

'And homeless.'

'And hasn't any food.'

We had all agreed and were pleased when the days went by and no one claimed her. Very quickly, Tigger, who was fast approaching adulthood, found an all-black male companion who persisted in following her around. I watched through the playroom window as he sat in the pouring rain, his long black fur sleeked against his sides, waiting for Tigger to appear.

When Tigger produced four tiny black, white and grey kittens, I was delighted. We all loved playing with them and watching the tiny creatures sprawling on splayed legs as they started to grow. But when they were old enough to go to new homes, we knew the kittens would be given away. While they were with us we each adopted a kitten, and as soon as the litter could lollop along the concrete path, Nigel, Stuart and I carried them out to the garden.

'We'll race them,' said Nigel, who had become our unofficial leader when David wasn't there.

A low wall ran along one side of the path and with the house on the other side it made a wide 'track' for the kittens to run along. We lined them up as best we could, holding them back until we felt their tiny bodies straining to be released.

'Ready, steady, go,' shouted Nigel, and we gave them their freedom. Some ran, some rolled and some just turned in the opposite direction. If two or three made a race of it we darted round them, shouting encouragement as we excitedly attracted our own kitten with trailing string and scraps of food.

Nigel and I were busily racing the kittens one day when we heard a knock on the front door. Mother was out, so reluctantly we popped the kittens back in their basket before opening the door.

An unknown man was standing there. 'Give this to your father,' he said, handing Nigel a long, heavy, black object, then he hurried away down the path, leaving us staring after him.

'It's a bomb!' said Nigel.

'It's not ticking.'

'They don't always tick.'

'What shall we do with it?'

'I'd better hide it.' And Nigel carried the 'bomb' into the hall, carefully placed it in the understairs cupboard and shut the door.

'Supposing it goes off?' I said. 'We can't keep it in the house.'

I stared at the cupboard door, wondering what would happen if the bomb exploded.

'I'll take it in the garden. It'll be safer there.' Cautiously Nigel opened the cupboard door again, picked up the long dark object and carried it out through the kitchen. He placed it under the fruit trees away from the house, until Mother returned and he told her what had happened.

'Whatever have you put it in the garden for?'

'In case it explodes.'

'Explodes! A baton can't *explode!* It's for the air raid wardens.'

'Baton?'

'Yes, to show Daddy's on duty tonight!'

Despite unofficial talk of the war ending the following year, air raids continued to batter London. They still came after dark and sometimes I heard a distant pounding gun or drone of an engine before the warning sounded. With this first hint of a raid I climbed out of bed in readiness. I didn't like to go down to the shelter until the siren started, in case the others thought I was a coward. But there was no harm in standing by my bed, ready to go as soon as the first whirrings began.

As I waited, I got into my dressing gown and slippers and pulled on my pink 'air raid trousers'. Mother had made these from thick, fleecy material, with elasticated waist and ankles, to wear over my nightdress for warmth. Nigel had a blue pair but he seldom remembered to put his on.

The whole business of getting up at night and going down to the shelter was a terrible intrusion for Nigel. Usually he had to be woken up and guided towards the landing. Even so, starting down the stairs didn't mean he would arrive at the shelter, and quite often he would turn round and go back up again in his sleep.

'Where's Nigel?' someone would say, and Mother would dash upstairs and find him fast asleep in bed.

I was quite different. The moment I detected a distant siren I headed for the stairs. Almost at once another siren followed, then another as each area took up the call in an ominous night chorus. If I hadn't heard a distant gun before the warning, I would be out of bed in a flash, into my air raid trousers and walking my feet into my slippers as I left the room, pulling on my dressing gown as I went.

There was a safety gate at the top of the stairs from the previous owners. It was normally kept shut, but when it was open it acted as a gate across my doorway. Either way, the gate had to be negotiated before I could be safely on my way down the stairs to the Morrison shelter.

Once everyone was inside we lay there listening to the drawn-out twang of guns, like expanding elastic that suddenly snapped. Gradually, distant sounds were overlaid by bursts from nearer guns splitting the air, and the guttural drone of German planes coming closer and closer. When a raid was particularly noisy, I lay with my teeth tightly clenched against my 'biting pillow'. I had heard, somewhere, that biting a small wad of material prevented the tongue from being bitten in severe bomb blast, so I found a small doll's pillow to bite.

If a raid lasted beyond midnight, children were allowed to go to school an hour late — much to our delight. At first Mother had taken me, but soon I got used to walking down Burbage Road, along Half Moon Lane, under Herne Hill railway bridge to catch a number 2 or 68 bus, or even one of the swaying metallic-smelling trams that rattled their way along Norwood Road.

The bus or tram ride took me along by Brockwell Park to Trinity Rise. I walked halfway up Trinity Rise to a large round water tank bulging in the school's side entrance. EWS I would read, painted on the side in large white letters. David told me it meant 'Emergency Water Supply', and was used for fire-fighting, but the sides were too high for me to look over. Then on up I would go, past the vegetable garden that had once been flower beds, past the tennis and netball courts to the school's back entrance and lower cloakroom, with its rows of pegs and hanging shoe bags.

I often heard the name Leatherhead mentioned at school, but at first I had little idea what it meant. Gradually I learned that at the start of the war most of the girls from St Martin's had been evacuated to Leatherhead, where they shared the buildings of St John's, a boys' boarding school.

The boys had lessons in the mornings and 'the brown school', as St Martin's was called because of the uniform, had lessons in the afternoon. When the school at Tulse Hill had reopened for girls who weren't evacuated, some senior school staff taught at both schools. In the mornings they were at Tulse Hill, then each afternoon they travelled by train to Leatherhead.

By the time I started, in September 1943, 'Leatherhead' was an intrinsic part of the school, so I began to hear more about it. I laughed when I heard that a prefect walked along the corridors, tinkling a triangle when each lesson ended. But school bells, like church bells, had been banned; ringing them would mean invasion.

That first uncertain autumn, as I worked my way towards Christmas, I had much to get used to. The four-storey building appeared massive to me, compared with Oakleigh House. And here were more high ceilings and tall windows, with deep low sills we were forbidden to stand on.

Each morning, we stood in a circle in the gym singing hymns. I liked 'All Things Bright and Beautiful' and 'We Plough the Fields and Scatter' best and soon learnt the words. We knelt and prayed and sat cross-legged on the floor while notices were read out, then in an orderly line we filed out of the gym and climbed the concrete stairs to our classrooms. At lunch time we crowded into the cookery room for school dinners at 4d a day, instead of having them in the main hall with the seniors. And there were my new friends, Mary Marsh and Gloria Gorringe.

At playtime we played 'tag' and 'release' or sometimes 'grandmother's footsteps'. If someone had a piece of string we made 'cat's cradles', weaving intricate patterns on our fingers. Or we crouched on the ground to throw and catch our five-stones. Before we were stopped we had battles with riders and 'horses', but our battles were far too boisterous for young ladies, we were told, so we looked for other games to play.

St Martin-in-the-Fields High School

As Christmas approached and the weather grew colder, we tried to protect our chilblained toes, which grew pink and puffy, and were painful to touch. Sometimes we wore gloves in the classroom, for there was little heating in schools. Even so, I was surprised when David told me that his class had to put on outdoor coats and run round the playing fields at intervals during their lessons to get warm.

But the cold, damp weather didn't stop 'Devizes' activities at home, and soon we had a whole town full of people, conjured up from the depths of fantasy. Mr Plynnyglyn; Patrick Damptiedar; C.K. Cox, the Chief of Police; and Horace Dixon, Chief Clerk to the Devizes Borough Council's Highways Department, were all David's inventions, although he was far more interested in organising than involving himself in day-to-day affairs. Nigel had become Robert Butterfield from Hencher Road; his rebel son Kenneth, the window cleaner; Michael Ackland and Mr Owen. While I was equally happy as Frank and Mary Nottingham from Portsmouth Avenue; or the Fangsters — Alfred, Norman and Hilary — and many more.

One weekend as I watched Father building a coal bunker from breeze blocks on to the side of the garage, I decided it would make a perfect site for 'Hawkins School'. Instantly I became Mrs Hawkins, the headmistress, modelling my school on Oakleigh House. Attached to it, a larger bunker for coke became the rougher 'Black and White School', and on rainy days I let my imagination run wild when I sat in the playroom drawing pictures of children hanging from broken windows or sliding down the dilapidated roof.

With little room to play in the coal bunker, I usually set up Hawkins School in the playroom with my collection of toy animals, Belinda my favourite doll and the blackboard and easel Grandpa had given me one Christmas. But one day, when I found the coal bunker empty, I arranged the toys on the black dust. Hardly had I started their lessons when I felt large warning spots of rain, so gathering up my school I ran back to the playroom.

A few days later I searched and searched for my matching green-check frogs. The two 'pupils' at Hawkins School had been favourites the moment Auntie Madge had made them for my birthday, but now I couldn't find them anywhere.

'Has anyone seen my green frogs?' I said, going from room to room. Then remembering the coal bunker I dashed outside, and there, heaped in a corner, lay the soaking wet bedraggled frogs. I took them indoors and spread them out to dry in my bedroom, but when I noticed them a day or so later they looked alarmingly different.

'Look, they're bigger,' I said to David, in surprise. 'Sort of bloated out.'

'They've gone mouldy that's why,' he said, picking up the frogs. 'And they're sprouting!'

'Sprouting? What do you mean?'

'They were filled with dried peas!'

Sadly my poor frogs had to be thrown away.

Reading was still a problem for me, so Mother sat with me in the playroom as we worked our way through stories — *Alice in Wonderland, The Wind in the Willows,* the Pooh stories,*Worzel Gummidge* and even *Cranford* by Mrs Gaskell, which I thought very grown-up. First Mother read a paragraph, then I laboured through the next.

'When Auntie Flo and Auntie Madge open the bookshop, there'll be lots of new books for you to read,' Mother said, encouragingly.

It seemed a strange time for the aunts to open a bookshop, with all the wartime economies, but newspapers had been cut in size with sometimes as few as four pages. And as each one was filled with news of the latest raids on a town 'somewhere in England', or of battle reports from abroad, books had become an antidote to this incessant war news.

After many months of waiting, the Board of Trade eventually granted the bookshop a licence in February 1944. By this time Auntie Flo had returned to a former secretarial post with the Crown Agents for the Colonies at Millbank in London. Auntie Madge was often on ambulance duty, or speeding through the village for the WVS on her ancient, over-large bicycle, so Mother agreed to look after the bookshop whenever she was needed. This meant that quite often I would be there too.

The double-fronted, bay-windowed shop at the bottom of Calton Avenue looked impressive to me. The door bell clanged when we trooped inside and I looked round at the bare shelves lining the walls from floor to ceiling. Two thirds of the left-hand wall would house an adults' lending library, and to my delight part of the remainder of that side had shelves for a children's library. The whole of the right-hand wall was ready for new books.

When the first parcels arrived from the publishers we all helped unpack them. There was no heating in the shop, so wearing thick winter coats we knelt on the floor and delved into each package to see what it contained.

'Here's another cookery book.'

'Look at this one. Is it fiction?'

'Where do you want the children's books?'

I was in my element; I had never seen so many books before. Even so, there were not enough to fill all the shelves because the shortage of paper meant fewer books were being printed, so there were 'quotas' from the publishers. To help cover the space, we opened up some of the books and spread them out along the shelves.

Many, I noticed, were on flimsy, discoloured paper with close small print and cheap bindings. But some had a lingering smell of crisp new paper and print, and even the wartime editions held a fascination for me.

To make thicker, stronger paper, Auntie Madge told me, a massive book drive had been organised the previous year, when fifty-six million books were collected throughout the country. Although some of these were distributed through a 'Books for the Forces' scheme and some went to libraries to replace those lost in air raids, most were re-pulped to make more new paper — and in time more new books. And some books had been specially designed to use paper off-cuts.

'Bertie the Barrage Balloon,' I read, picking up a tiny narrow book. I liked the shape and all the illustrations, so I bought *Bertie the Barrage Balloon* with my pocket money.

Jutting out diagonally, just in front of the children's library, stood the main counter — a heavy table from Glenshee House School. I examined the flat wooden till resting on the counter, and the bell 'tinged' as the narrow cash drawer clicked open, moving the till roll on to a blank space for the next sale to be written in.

On the counter, too, were book marks, gift tags and small displays. Later, in the summer, I would bunch up sprays of lavender from the garden, to sell in aid of the Red Cross or RSPCA. I was never allowed to sell things for myself, however desperately I needed the money. Just as at Christmas, money from our carol singing had to be given to a good cause. But there were always plenty of charities to choose from: Prisoners of War; Aid to China; Children from Occupied Countries; the Red Cross 'Penny-a-week', and special campaigns to raise money for aircraft, tanks or ships.

Air raids had tailed off by the end of 1943, but just when the bookshop was being nurtured through its tentative opening weeks, London experienced a 'mini blitz'. Raids still came at night, but even so Father dragged a spare mattress into the understairs cupboard, behind the children's library, so that if a daytime warning did sound anyone in the shop could dive into the cupboard.

One morning, towards the end of March I toiled up Trinity Rise, late after yet another all-night raid. Ahead I saw a knot of girls standing by the static water tank at the side entrance to the school. As I drew near I sensed a buzz of excitement and could see the stocky figure of Miss Orme by the gate. She was turning girls away, so I hurried up the hill to see what had happened.

'The school's been bombed!' someone said.

With a mixture of shock and excitement I learned that the top floor was badly damaged by fire. Water had streamed through the building and down across the netball courts, forming a lake on the lower court. It was just another bomb — but this one affected me.

We all returned home that day and stayed home for the next six weeks. By the beginning of May the damaged top floor had been made temporarily safe, but it remained out of bounds, so only the senior school crowded back to usable parts of the building. With no room for the Preparatory Department, we crowded round a large table at the back of Trinity Rise church each morning, while stern-looking, but kind-hearted, Mrs Davies fired questions at us in quick succession.

'Five elevens?'

'Fifty-five.'

'Seven elevens?'

'Seventy-seven.'

'Eleven elevens?

'Eleventy-eleven!' came an over-enthusiastic reply.

We had general knowledge quizzes, too, but it was difficult in the cramped conditions with few books, and soon our lessons stopped.

It had been David's idea earlier in the year to start the DVS. He said he was the leader and Nigel could be the vice captain. I became a corporal and Stuart a private.

'What does DVS mean?' I had asked.

'Dulwich Victory Scouts, of course.'

'What're we going to do?'

'Training.'

Training sounded fun, especially as the war meant we didn't belong to any outside clubs. As part of our training, one Saturday afternoon David marched us up to Sydenham Hill to watch a game of football. We then marched back down to Dulwich Park to play our own match. Afterwards David proudly reported the afternoon's event in the *DVS Magazine*.

'I'm only going to make one copy each month,' he said, as he painstakingly wrote the sixteen-page magazine in four different coloured inks. 'Grandma and the aunts can see it later.'

David wrote a serial story and news items for the magazine, and Nigel made up a junior crossword. I was pleased when my picture puzzle and jumbled words appeared in the Puzzle Corner, and David thanked *Mr S.A. Green of Dulwich* for sending in a main crossword.

At an early meeting, we sat round the playroom table discussing important business, when the job of treasurer was transferred from David to Nigel. Nigel had complained that David was in charge of

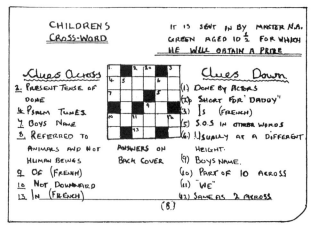

Nigel made up a junior crossword

everything, so David made several promotions, too. Private S. Macpherson was upgraded to lance corporal; Corporal M. Green to sergeant and also editor's secretary; and Vice Captain N. Green became the Divisional Captain.

'I'll be the Salvage Officer as well,' Nigel had said, when he heard about the promotions.

It was important to have a Salvage Officer in the DVS, because every area had one, and at school we were encouraged to collect all kinds of unlikely things to be re-used for the 'war effort'. So David had given details of our own salvage efforts in a GENERAL NOTICES section of the magazine:

As you know we are aiming to collect 5 pounds of rubber by the 29th February. We have so far collected approx.1¹/₄ lbs which, as the Salvage Officer says, is not enough. So please, all our readers, send as much rubber or milk tops (tin foil) silver paper or bones to Nigel Green, Salvage Officer, DVS. Thank you.

Under the heading THINGS WE HAVE HEARD, David wrote:

We were very proud to hear that Miss Madeline Green did some gallant work while saving the lives of a number of bombed people in the Camberwell area during a recent London raid.

He copied the expression *a recent London raid* from wireless and newspaper reports, which were not allowed to give specific details. While David sat at one end of the playroom table, busily writing the magazine, I sat at the other end laboriously winding raffia around two circles of card.

'Can I put an advert in the magazine?' I said.

'What's it for?'

'Two raffia dinner mats.'

'Let's see them.'

After examining the mats David agreed that I could, and he added a green and red illustration. *They are 4-inches in diameter,* the advertisement read, *and going at moderate prices. Apply Miss M. Green aged 9. Box A.Y. DVS Magazine.*

Although DVS activities and the magazine took up some of our spare time, our world of Devizes still continued unabated. But now talk of the war ending before Christmas had begun again, so on the 6th June, when the much planned D-Day landing was finally launched, it became even more likely.

'It's D-Day! It's D-Day!' we all shouted, thinking the war was almost over.

The one o'clock news started 'D-Day. *The* Day' and told of the build-up towards this longed-for attack. All along the south coast, troops, guns and equipment, ships and landing craft had been assembling. Even dummy ships, planes and tanks had been planted at various non-strategic places to confuse the enemy.

But the beaches east of Cherbourg were the real battleground. Two days later we heard recorded accounts of the Normandy landings, and every news and extra war bulletin told of the progress; some with graphic recordings of sounds of battle brought into our homes for the first time. It looked at last as though the hard-fought war would soon be over.

Yet, only one week after D-Day we saw a strange sight moving across the sky. It was accompanied by an unnerving, clattering throb. We had no idea what it was, or that we were about to experience the final, devastating phase of the war in Europe.

7. Flying Bombs and V2s: 1944-1945

'Listen to that milk cart clattering down the road,' said Mother, as we huddled together in the Morrison shelter. 'Whatever is it doing out at this time of night?' When the 'milk cart' suddenly stopped we didn't immediately connect the brief silence with the loud explosion that followed.

It was the middle of June, and two days later we watched a dark cylindrical shape, with squared-off wings, move across the sky. Flames were shooting from a pod on its back.

A dark cylindrical shape in the sky

'It's on fire!' shouted David, and we all cheered, thinking it was a crippled German plane. But the slight uptilt of its drone as the engine cut, the momentary silence, the horrific drawn-out rumbling explosion were soon to become frighteningly familiar.

Now, suddenly, air raid warnings were coming in the daytime as well as at night, and no sooner had one all-clear sounded than the next warning shrilled out. Sometimes we saw several black specks streaking across the sky as these sinister objects approached.

But after a few days we realised that an unnerving silence surrounded the approaching planes, for the boom of anti-aircraft guns protecting London had stopped. We had no way of knowing that shooting down this pilotless, secret weapon caused as much devastation as when it dived to the ground and exploded, so hearing the threatening sounds without the protective guns made us feel totally vulnerable. And we were completely unaware that many of these strange machines were being shot down before they reached London, mostly exploding in Kent or Sussex.

To me it was all part of the war, but because there were so many air raid warnings Nigel and I slept in the Morrison shelter. Now I no longer listened so acutely for the hint of distant drones, ready to leap out of bed and rush downstairs. My only fear was that David and my parents might not get there in time. But sometimes they stayed on in the shelter when the night was heavy with sirens, and at other times Father was on duty as an air raid warden or special constable in the police.

I didn't mind being cooped up in the shelter, because Nigel and I played guessing games.

'Let's play *I Know Somebody,*' one of us would say, and we took turns to describe someone in minute detail for the other to identify.

When we tired of *I Know Somebody,* we tapped out the beat of a tune on each other's back.

'It's like something I know, but you're not doing it right,' I said.

'How d'you know it's not right if you don't know what it is?'

'It should go like this.' And I tapped out another tune.

'No it shouldn't. This is how it goes. I should know, I thought of it.' More tapping ensued, but it kept our minds off the reason we were in the shelter.

One bonus for me was that St Martin's remained closed, firstly because of the bomb damage and now because of this latest threat. The only exception was for girls taking School Certificate and Matriculation exams. But David and Nigel had no such holiday, so school for them continued with frequent dashes to the shelter. Sometimes this was impossible when a pilotless aircraft slipped through before a warning could sound.

Newspapers and the wireless only mentioned 'incidents' in 'Southern England', so it was some time before the full horror of what was happening seeped out. By then, names such as 'flying bomb', 'doodlebug' and 'buzz bomb' were being used to describe Germany's V1, vengeance weapon, but it didn't make them any less sinister.

Just before the doodlebugs started, Tigger had produced a second litter of kittens. Three months after her first litter, friends who had asked for a fluffy, long-haired tabby, found they didn't really want him. So 'Fluff' had returned to us, a soft, perfumed bundle of neutered fur.

Now, when Tigger was away from her bed in the understairs cupboard, Fluff would climb in, settle down with the tiny furry bundles and start to wash and care for them. He left when Tigger returned, but good-natured Fluff soon took over the job of caring more permanently, and during the day Tigger was perfectly happy leaving it to him. As the kittens grew and started wandering on shaky legs, we settled them in a large wicker laundry basket at night and slid it under the kitchen table as added protection.

Tigger

'Good-night, kittens. Good-night, Tigger,' I said one evening, peeping into their basket.

I ran upstairs to get undressed, but hardly had I reached my room when the stomach-churning siren started up. I was searching in my dressing table and had pulled both drawers out, but the previous winter the wood had swollen and slightly distorted, so the drawers jammed when I hastily tried to push them back. I pulled roughly at each one, hoping to free them, but they still stuck fast. The siren was wailing and already I should be on my way down the stairs. With one final tug, I left the drawers half open and hurried down to the shelter.

Mother, Nigel and I huddled at one end, with Father and David squashed at our feet by the entrance. Fluff crawled in to curl up on the blankets before the end panel was clipped on, and we lay there, listening to the threatening sounds we knew so well. As each deep-throated rattle grew louder, I shut my eyes hoping the dreaded engine would pass overhead before it cut out. And with every terrifying explosion we tried to estimate where it might be.

Towards early morning I heard a distant clatter becoming persistently louder and deeper, losing height as it kept on coming. Locked in our own private thoughts, no one spoke. It was so close now it sounded almost overhead. 'Please, please keep on going,' I whispered.

But I heard the slight uptilt as the engine cut and with a sudden, eerie crack of branches it clipped the oak tree in the allotment at the end of the garden. I buried my head under my pillow as a rush of air swooped down, immediately followed by a reverberating, crashing, glass-shattering roar. As the last rumblings died away, something clattered somewhere in the house, and slowly I raised my head.

Peering through the caged side of the shelter, I could see the playroom was intact; no windows were broken; the ceiling was still secure. We were alive. As soon as it was safe to do so, Father unclipped the end panel and climbed out to see what had happened. I heard a distant sound of engines, then from the hall Father called out to make sure we put on slippers or shoes.

I followed the others out of the shelter, and with a suppressed feeling of fear and excitement stood by the open playroom door. The hall was a mess. Brightening morning light shone through the space where the front door had been; the once-solid door and the inner porch doors now lay in splinters of jagged wood and glass.

With great care I climbed over the chaos, and made my way after the others through the open space to the front garden. Here, broken tiles and more glass were strewn over the paths and lawn. We stared in silence, standing there in the crisp morning air as the first faint notes of all-clear started up. Other all-clear sirens followed, each wailing reaching its crescendo in succession.

Stepping clear of the debris we straggled to the lopsided garden gates, where one drooped on a single hinge. I looked beyond the cross roads, hardly noticing the group of people standing on the pavement, with wardens coming and going, or the tangle of hose pipes lying in the road. I only saw stark white trees at intervals down the road, as though a heavy covering of snow had just fallen. From the gateway the sight of the demolished house was hidden, so I stared, amazed by the dust-covered trees. And the picture stayed with me.

The sounds of all-clear gradually died away as more neighbours came from their houses. But my ears were attuned to listen, in case a doodlebug slipped through without warning.

We soon learned that Barbara, the daughter of the house that received the direct hit, had worked late. Being over-tired she had decided to sleep on the settee, instead of with her parents in the cramped Anderson shelter in the garden. Barbara had been killed outright; but her parents were rescued. We didn't know the family, even so I felt a sick unease as I listened to the details. If only she had gone to the shelter.

Turning from the gate, we looked at our own house. The force of the blast had been siphoned across to our corner, leaving gaping holes in the roof where tiles had been torn off, as though a giant hand had plucked them at random. And we saw shattered windows and damage everywhere. As we stood there, a bird started to sing. Others chirped back. Their song grew louder, filling the air. Birds in their innocence knew nothing of man's inhumanity. It was just another day.

Back in the house we made straight for the kitchen. I lifted the lid of the laundry basket and peered inside.

'Tigger, you're all right!' I said, as she climbed out, leaving her five tiny kittens sleeping contentedly.

'Keep the door shut,' said Mother. 'We don't want Tigger in the hall with all that glass. Where's Fluff?'

'Still in the shelter.'

'We'd better see what the other rooms are like.'

We left the kitchen, carefully shutting the door, and followed Father up the stairs. I looked up at the slatted laths above the landing, as early morning light filtered in, and I felt my slippered feet crunching on pieces of fallen ceiling. Looking into each bedroom we saw more chunks of plaster and broken glass littering the furniture and floors. And I saw the thick layer of dust and plaster, now covering the crumpled clothes in my open dressing table drawers.

I grew used to seeing the gaps in the ceilings, with their striped laths showing through, and the fine dust that blew down from the jagged plaster. Ceilings, I knew, were classed as 'non-essential war damage', which meant they wouldn't be repaired until after the war. But then again, we had been lucky; we had survived.

'More buckets,' called Mother, when rain dripped through the roof, before it was repaired. So we had buckets on the landing to collect the worst of the rain.

The following month, in the early hours of the morning, a direct hit on Dulwich Picture Gallery sent its blast straight across the playing fields to the back of our house. We were being buffeted from both directions. But this time, being further away, the damage was less severe.

When the doodlebugs began, the DVS with its magazines and activities had abruptly stopped, although 'Devizes' carried on. If we were playing in the garden and a flying bomb headed our way, we dashed for the shelter calling our mother as we ran. But the moment the all-clear sounded we continued as before.

'We can use the garage doors as a wicket,' said Nigel, temporarily relinquishing his guise as Kenneth Butterfield or Michael Ackland, when they were playing cricket with Frank Nottingham and Norman Fangster.

'And we can pretend we're on Devizes Meadow,' I said. 'After all we can't really play cricket in Cert Street.'

Occasionally Norman Fangster's brother, Alfred, would be persuaded to play, but his limp presented problems. And sometimes we pretended that Dennis Compton, Len Hutton, the Bedser twins and other well-known cricketers made surprise guest appearances.

While we lived in our all-consuming Devizes world, we had no way of knowing how the war was affecting other parts of the country, or even other parts of London, because the Ministry of Information had imposed a strict ban on reporting individual incidents. Even so, word went round telling of this terrifying new weapon, and how the immense blast from the explosion was causing more death and damage.

I knew we were discouraged from discussing the effects of the war with other people, for fear of information leaking to the enemy, and I had seen slogans such as 'Careless Talk Costs Lives', with their funny cartoon pictures. But surely the war would soon be over? Everyone *knew* that, so I couldn't understand why we weren't allowed to talk about what was happening.

One reason for suppressing the details — although we had no idea — was because many V1 flying bombs were falling short of their target. South of the Thames had the greatest number, with the mean point of impact proving to be Dulwich instead of Charing Cross. We had no idea, either, about the involved scheme being put forward, to pass false information to the Germans.

The ingenious plan, devised by MI6, was to feed back information saying the V1s were going *beyond* their target, in the hope that the

CARELESS TALK COSTS LIVES

range would be shortened. Many V1s would then fall further south in less densely populated areas. Instead, news reached Germany that V1s were landing *on* target, so the MPI remained the same — Dulwich. But as a result the City was less severely battered than it would otherwise have been.

'Dulwich College has been hit!' said David, hurrying into the kitchen from school one lunch time. 'They can't do the school cert there now. It's too badly damaged.'

Surprisingly, despite the ban on publicity, the following week we read about the incident in a local newspaper. The story was quickly picked up by a German newspaper which added that the college was being used as a 'temporary military headquarters'. Although this was untrue, there were 'temporary military headquarters' nearby, because the Dutch government-in-exile had secretly leased a large house at Dulwich Common to train agents. The agents were then parachuted into Holland to help the Dutch resistance and keep in radio contact with Britain. We, of course, knew nothing about them, and the V1 on Dulwich College was, like all the others, a random incident.

'These wretched things are still coming over,' Mother said, as we stood in the garden looking to the sky. 'I do think we should be told exactly what's happening.'

News bulletins were full of victories after the Normandy landings, as Allied forces continued their thrust forward. Despite some set-backs, with battles raging to and fro, we heard of cheering, flag-waving crowds freed at last from years of oppression. News further north was also encouraging as Russia continued to gain ground. But nothing was said of the V1 pilotless aircraft.

After three weeks of rumours, Winston Churchill announced to parliament that London was the chief target for the new weapon. To our amazement we learned that between 100 and 150 flying bombs, each weighing one ton, were being launched every day. But we also heard that a large number either failed to cross the channel or were shot down before reaching London. Nevertheless, we were horrified that between 20 and 100 a day were falling mainly on South London.

Even with this announcement, partial censorship on the radio and in the newspapers continued, and incidents were referred to as 'a recent attack'. But now we could talk more openly about what was happening and at least build up a broader picture.

As the days of the V1 continued, we had to stay close to the house because of the frequency of air raid warnings. But once we became accustomed to the pattern of daytime doodlebugs we often watched them as they came over.

'Listen, I can hear one,' I said one day, as Nigel and I were engrossed with Devizes in the garden, while Mother was at the bookshop. 'There it is!'

'It's not coming this way,' said Nigel, watching its steady flight.

But as he spoke, the clattering engine cut, the nose dipped down and we dived for cover under the laurel bushes. A terrible roar split the air, and it felt as though the ground shook beneath us. Crawling out from the bushes, we looked up and saw a ghastly pall of grey smoke. It was frighteningly near, rising above the trees and rooftops.

'It's Herne Hill!' said Nigel.' And being Nigel, as soon as the all-clear sounded, he jumped on his bike and made a quick dash to see where the bomb had landed. 'Carver Road,' he reported back. 'The road's cordoned off, so I couldn't see much.'

One afternoon, a few days later, when Nigel had cycled off to North Dulwich to see a friend, the wailing siren began before he returned. With a tight, sick feeling I heard a V1 approaching. Then the juddering sound cut out and almost at once came the tremendous roar as the doodlebug exploded. But soon afterwards Nigel hurtled up the front path. His bike clattered on the gravel and he ran indoors.

'Did you see that one?' he said, excitedly. 'I was on my way home. I saw it coming over. It was there, right above me!'

He had leapt from his bike as a soldier dashed from a garden, grabbed him by the arm and shepherded him to safety between two houses. The inevitable crash and roar had hardly rumbled away before Nigel pedalled furiously for home.

At night we occasionally stood by the playroom door watching a doodlebug's tail of flame moving across the sky. But we soon dived into the shelter if we thought it was coming our way. Lying on the mattress I would bite on my biting pillow, listening to the unmistakable engine growing louder.

'The milkman said so many people have left London he can let me have an extra pint,' I heard Mother say one morning. 'Do you think there'll be more coke now for the boiler?'

I knew when there was no coke for the little grey boiler in the kitchen, because there was no hot water. Instead, we boiled up a kettle to use in the hand basin. By standing on the edge of the bath I could get one foot at a time into the basin, and just in case a warning sounded I washed in two halves, dressing the first washed part before washing the second. Each morning before waiting for a kettle to boil, I used cold water. But one thing I had to remember was to put the plug in the basin so no water was wasted.

Washing my hair was another problem now my bunches had lengthened to plaits. Mother added a few drops of vinegar to the rinsing water to make my hair shine, and the cold water rinse — to 'close the pores' — came as a shock. In the winter I had hung my head down in front of the playroom fire, feeling its drying warmth, but now without a fire my hair stayed wet. I always hoped no doodlebugs would come over until we had finished the business of hair washing.

Rumours reported that over a million people had left London because of the V1s. Those who were left carried on working, maintaining that as no one knew where or when one would land it made no difference. Auntie Madge told us that spotters were posted on office and factory rooftops to warn when a V1 was approaching, And people tried not to be on the streets for too long, but if caught at the start of a warning, they made for the nearest shelter to escape from the blast. Shops in many areas closed down, too, but shopping still had to be done, flying bombs or no flying bombs. And there was always a queue.

'Take cover!' someone would shout, if a V1 came too close. Then the queue scuttled into doorways.

Unbeknown to us the full effects of the anti-V1 tactics was beginning to be felt. Four days before 'our' doodlebug in Burbage Road, a barrage of balloons had been set up in a semi-circle along the North Downs, and a line of anti-aircraft guns had been positioned further south.

By August an even denser barrage stretched from Redhill to Chatham. While along the coast between Beachy Head and Dover, rocket launchers and batteries of anti-aircraft guns, guided by radar, were blasting away at approaching V1s. Fighters patrolled over the Channel, endeavouring to bring their speedy targets spiralling into the water. And sometimes they managed to tip the wings of a V1 and send it back.

Listening to the BBC News, we heard of V1 launch-sites being repeatedly bombed, and of those still in action being overrun by advancing Allied troops. Yet, despite all this, many V1s continued to reach London right up to the beginning of September, when suddenly, for the first time for many weeks, no flying bombs came.

We cheered, thinking the war was almost over, and many people started returning to London. But after a week of silence V1s came again, this time approaching from the east and scattering over a wider area. They were being launched from Heinkels flying low across the sea, and although we didn't realise it in early autumn 1944, they were to continue spasmodically until the following spring.

I started back at St Martin's in September, after spending not just the holidays at home but the whole of the summer term, too. Dressed in my thick winter uniform, although the weather was still warm, I climbed the path by the netball courts to join a throng of girls, their chattering voices telling of their experiences through the long summer months of doodlebugs. And with a strange, uncertain feeling I looked for familiar faces while we waited for the school doors to open.

Once inside, a penetrating pungence clung to the building, reminding me of the wet, burnt smell after our incendiary bomb in Swansea. As I climbed the concrete stairs to find a place in my new classroom, the smell grew stronger. I saw an 'out of bounds' notice further up the staircase, and realised the laboratories and art room were still dangerous after being gutted by fire.

Before a hierarchy developed of where to sit and who to sit with, I unwittingly became door monitor when I chose the desk nearest the door. For that term, whenever an adult or prefect came into the classroom, I would have to leap up ready to open and close the door. If our regal headmistress Miss Gordon Ewen — or any member of staff — came into the room, the whole class stood until we were motioned to sit down again.

Being door monitor was quite important, I thought, but joint milk monitor with Mary Marsh would be far more fun. Just before break each morning the milk monitors escaped from the lesson to count out third-pint bottles, and with a pencil poked a hole in each lid for the straw, before carrying the crate up the concrete stairs to the classroom. Next term I'll be milk monitor, I told myself.

Although I knew there could still be air raids, before I returned to school we had heard encouraging news of Allied advances, and the liberation of Paris, Marseilles, Brussels and Antwerp. So we really did believe the war was about to end.

But Friday the 8th September dashed our hopes.

On that wet September evening a gigantic explosion shattered the silence. It came from the direction of Chiswick. Almost immediately came a second explosion from somewhere near Epping. At first, as there had been no warning, it sounded like a gas works exploding or possibly a delayed bomb; or even damaged, unsafe buildings being blown up. Many rumours circulated, but by the time we heard one or two of these explosions each day, a new German secret weapon was suspected.

Sitting on the swing in my nightdress, on a drier evening a few days later, I pushed off with my bare feet from the patch of worn grass. Nearby my parents sat in deck chairs, talking. As I swung idly to and fro, I caught snatches of their conversation. Something about moving away and where could we go?

I listened, but my own thoughts took over. Move away from Dulwich? But this was our home. How could we move away? The doodlebugs were almost over, so why move now?

But my parents realised a greater threat had arrived. Although the press silence remained, details soon circulated of the sudden, catastrophic devastation caused by the new weapon. There was no warning, but a double supersonic bang could be heard, immediately followed by a horrendous explosion that persisted in a long drawn-out roar, louder and longer than a V1.

The new weapon penetrated deep into the ground, creating a huge crater, with earthquake reverberations spiralling outwards like a stone dropped into a pond. The result was flattened homes and extensive damage. One minute buildings, buses, roads, trees — and people — were intact, the next they had gone.

Twenty-five such explosions occurred in the first nine days of the onslaught. The next day, the twenty-sixth demolished a church in West Norwood, barely a mile away from us. Each time these shattering explosions occurred, the same feeling of fear plummeted inside me. I looked to the sky for the telltale pall of smoke, trying to estimate where it might be, and silently realising the next one could be nearer.

Newspapers said nothing. A total press blackout had once more been enforced, because if no mention was made of the new weapon landing, the enemy might think it hadn't reached London.

So once again we wondered; rumours were rife; no one really knew.

Although to us this frightening phase of the war had suddenly erupted, the government had been aware of fragmentary reports, as early as 1943, which told of a possible supersonic rocket. By June of that year, while we were still in Beckenham planning to move to South London — and thinking nothing could be worse than the blitz on Swansea — the Ministry for Home Security was already estimating that a large area of London, including Dulwich, could expect to be devastated without prior warning. The only counter-measure available was to try to destroy all factories and launch sights. But this proved to be only partially successful.

On the evening I was happily swinging and my parents were discussing the possibility of moving away, they knew only that an even more destructive weapon was landing. But there was a lull for a week when no V2 rockets came. Everyone hoped the bridgehead at Arnhem would soon end the war, or at least liberate Holland where many launch sites were thought to be.

Sadly we heard that the Arnhem bridgehead was not successful, so the V2 lull did not last long. Yet still the press silence remained, even though up to five rockets were reaching England each day. Newspapers were full of morale-boosting details of incidents abroad, but the cause of the gigantic explosions around us was not officially divulged.

Finally, on the 10th November, Winston Churchill made a statement to parliament about the V2 rockets. Now, at last, newspapers could report on what had been happening in London for the past two months, but as with the V1s, precise details were not given.

The most terrifying part, I thought, was the lack of warning. We didn't know where or when a rocket would land. It just happened. When a particularly close explosion erupted one day, David was minding the bookshop. I dashed into the garden to see where the pall of smoke and dust was rising, and from its position I knew David would be near by. Eventually David raced home on his bike, full of the story.

'There was a terrific roar and the shop windows just caved in,' he said, breathlessly. 'It's a terrible mess. Everything's covered in glass.'

He told us that in the split second before the V2 exploded, there had been an inexplicable sound and sensation, as though the air was being sucked away. In that moment he dived below the counter; the bay windows shattered and jagged glass spikes shot over his head, embedding themselves in the wall behind him. The V2 had landed in Court Lane, less than half a mile from the bookshop. Still talking about his lucky escape, David immediately returned to the shop with our parents, to help clear away the débris.

By foggy December, as the erratic autumn term, which I had mostly missed, came to an end, I had a strange mixture of feelings, because although rockets and doodlebugs continued to fall, hope of German surrender was mounting. The Home Guard had been disbanded and I knew events abroad were moving swiftly towards peace. Early in 1945, after a cheerful Christmas with extra meat and sweet rations and half a pound more sugar, we dared to think the war would soon be over. At the end of March, thankfully, the last of the V1s and V2s had fallen.

Then on the evening of the 1st May, sitting in the dining room listening to the BBC Home Service, we heard the most unexpected announcement. Hitler was reported to have committed suicide.

With this news the German fight collapsed and negotiations were started for their unconditional surrender. It came on the 7th May. Abruptly the months of waiting, of wondering how much longer the war could drag on, were over. The next day, VE Day — Victory in Europe Day — the whole country went wild.

And so did we.

8. Peace: 1945-1946

Church bells rang with joy in every city, town and village. People danced and sang in the streets as a sea of red, white and blue surged into the centre of London. Winston Churchill's speech was relayed to hushed crowds outside the Houses of Parliament, and King George V1 broadcast to the nation. There was sadness, too, much sadness, but the paramount feeling of happiness could not be suppressed.

An overwhelming sense of relief surged over me, as though a great weight had been lifted, and an unrealistic feeling took over. 'We needn't shut the curtains now, before we switch on the light,' I said. And I knew there would be no more nagging worries of 'will we survive?'.

I could hardly remember the time before the war, but suddenly life had changed. Strangers laughed and smiled; and we could think ahead. The BBC now relayed news of victory parties and celebrations all over the country, where streets were lined with bunting and flags. Auntie Gladys told us that she had hung out her enormous Union Jack — as she did on all patriotic occasions.

Hurrying past the V1 bomb site in Burbage Road, we joined laughing crowds lining the tiered seats around Herne Hill Cycle Track, to watch fireworks bursting and sparkling into life. By the weekend we had put up a long trestle table in the garden, and soon it was laden with saved-up food. Neighbours, Mrs Mac and Stuart, Grandma and the aunts all crowded in, bringing plates and bowls for this 'feast' to celebrate victory.

But while we celebrated, the BBC also reported heavy attacks by Japanese Kamikaze planes on the British Pacific fleet. War in the Far East was still as intense and still as brutal. Yet it would be many years before I understood the part the Far East played. 'My war' had been in Europe, against Germany, and that war was over. Later, on the 6th and 9th of August we would hear that atomic bombs had been dropped — finally to end World War 2.

Later still, on the 11th November at 11 o'clock, I would stand in silence with my family, as we listened to the commemoration service on the wireless; a ritual I was to observe each year because I knew people had died. But the horrors, the inhumanity, the destruction were too great for me to understand completely, for I hadn't learnt to look beyond the immediate.

We didn't mind rations being reduced now the war was over, because we knew vital supplies were needed in liberated countries where many people were starving. The horrific, emaciated conditions of those who survived concentration camps also came to light. And with soldiers and prisoners starting to return home, all needed a share of the decreasing stocks.

To eke out our own dwindling rations, occasionally at lunch time we walked or cycled with Mother to the Grafton Hall in Village Way, where basic communal meals were served.

'I wonder what we'll have,' called Nigel, speeding on ahead.

'Mmm, it smells good. It's a nice sort of food-smell. Not like Brynmill.' And I remembered, again, my anguish at lunchtime in the 'big' school in Wales.

Jostling in a queue with the others, I collected my soup, 'meat and two veg', sponge pudding and a cup of tea without a saucer. Then we sat at a small table to enjoy our shilling meals. 'British Restaurant' sounded a grand name for the old hall, but I liked watching the food being served and people coming and going. We hadn't come here during the war, because of air raids, but now we could sit at leisure and talk about the intricacies of Devizes, our flourishing imaginary world.

It seemed to me as though Devizes had always been there, with its police force, bank, tax office, schools, libraries, hospital and all our complex characters. It had just grown and grown and become more and more complete. But today, as we ate our meal and watched the different people, there were other things to think about besides Devizes. There was talk of going on a seaside holiday!

The sea for me meant Swansea, with its rolls of barbed wire stretched along the beach. I still had a vague memory of our pre-war holiday in the Isle of Wight when I was three. David said I got lost and was found wandering up a hill, but all I remembered was a vast expanse of sand and brightness, a beach hut, rocks with a natural spring trickling from the cliffs, and a strange, strong, tangy smell.

Then for the six war years no such luxuries as buckets and spades were made and all the amenities of seaside towns closed down. Some, like piers and kiosks, fell into disrepair. When the enormous task of defusing and clearing mines was finally completed in July, a sudden surge of holiday makers was expected to flock to seaside resorts for a different kind of invasion.

On Nigel's birthday, Saturday the 11th August, we squashed into a brown Buick taxi bound for Herne Hill Station. I still remembered standing there six years earlier, waiting to be evacuated to Patcham. And I still remembered our fateful all-day journey from Swansea to Beckenham. But now here we were setting off by train for a holiday by the sea.

Our parents had studied the map, and Lancing in Sussex seemed the nearest and most convenient place to reach. There had been no thought of special holiday clothes, with clothing coupons still in use. We simply packed a few of our everyday things in the big, pre-war leather suitcase and set off full of excited anticipation.

We rented a small bungalow called Wayfarers, beyond a level crossing where we stopped to watch the occasional train, when we walked down to the beach. It was a stony beach, but I didn't mind as I carefully trod, step-by-step over the rounded pebbles, following the boys down to the water. Mother sat in a deck chair, surrounded by clothes, towels and the picnic, while Father swam.

'I'll give 2s 6d to the first one who learns to swim,' he said, as we splashed and spluttered around him.

Some days we caught a bus into Worthing and walked along the sea-front, fascinated by the surging waves pounding and battering each breakwater.

'Look at that spray!' shouted David, above the roar of the wind that muffled our ears.

I watched the tiny silver droplets spewing from the tumbling water and marvelled at the high-pitched screeching seagulls, swooping and diving overhead. And I breathed once more the tangy smell of seaweed.

One day as we walked back to the bungalow, Father suggested we collected small pebbles for a game of 'housey-housey'. We used the pebbles as counters on his neatly written number cards. I enjoyed our evenings of homemade games. They were all part of the holiday.

When Nigel and I set off for the beach one morning, over the level crossing and along to South Street, we saw an unfamiliar notice outside a small tobacconist.

'Ice cream!' said Nigel. 'Come on, let's have one.' And he pushed open the door, starting the bell jangling.

I followed him into the shop where we each bought a 1d cone. Standing outside, we savoured this rare luxury, until the last squashy point had disappeared. Then we carried on down the shop-lined road, looking in all the windows.

'Look, there's another ice cream sign,' I said. 'Shall we have another one?'

There had been no ice cream during the war, so there and then we decided to buy an ice cream in every shop we came to on our way to the beach. Sometimes we bought 1d cones, but sometimes 2d cones were the cheapest we could buy, and our limited pocket money was fast running out. By the time we reached the sea I was almost relieved there were no more shops; we had bought fourteen ice cream cones and eaten seven each.

It started to rain the next day as we all travelled by bus along the sea-front to Worthing. 'We could go to the pictures,' someone suggested, and my spirits rose.

In Swansea, David and Nigel had occasionally gone to see a film at the Maxine Cinema in Gower Road, but I hadn't been allowed to go. So now, with The *Diamond Horseshoe* about to start its afternoon performance, we hurried into the warm, dry cinema, shuffled into our plush seats and waited expectantly. As the lights dimmed and the curtain lifted, brilliant lights, dazzling colours, resounding music and singing seemed to burst from the screen. I was overwhelmed by this glamorous world I had previously missed, and an intense feeling of excitement surged through me.

On another wet outing to Worthing, after wandering round the shops, my parents bought a full-sized xylophone on a sturdy wooden frame. I couldn't think why they wanted to buy such an unusual instrument, but I longed to try it as we carried the ungainly package back on the bus to Lancing. But the xylophone had to stay in its box, waiting to be assembled when we were back at home.

'There's going to be a bonfire tonight,' said Nigel, finding us all in the small kitchen. 'Can we go and see it?'

'It's for VJ Day,' David said. 'I saw them getting it ready.'

'What's VJ Day?'

'Victory over Japan, silly.' David often called me 'silly', when I asked naive questions.

That evening we crossed the level crossing and trooped down to the beach for the celebrations. But to me it was just a bonfire. My war had ended back in May, when people laughed and cheered, and the strain had suddenly lifted.

Like all holidays, our stay at the seaside was soon over, and we struggled back by train with the xylophone. We were full of memories of the sound of waves spilling and splashing over the stony beach, and the incessant screeching of seagulls. David won the 2s 6d for learning to swim, although Nigel and I were suspicious of his jerky movements.

'He looked like he was pushing one foot off the bottom all the time,' said Nigel. And I agreed.

When I saw David and his friend George McDonald digging at the bottom of the garden one day, I went to investigate. They were in the small triangular area behind a hedge, where weeds were dumped and woody bonfires could smoulder. Nigel was digging too, shovelling the earth into buckets.

'What are you doing?'

'Here, empty this,' said David, ignoring my question and handing me a bucket. 'Over there in the corner.'

So I emptied the buckets, one after the other, while the boys dug. When the hole was deep and wide enough, David and George took turns to dig away on one side.

'The earth's crumbling,' came a muffled voice. 'We'll have to shore it up.'

After further examination, Nigel and I were sent to 'acquire' planks of wood from a bomb-damaged house next-door-but-one. We set off, squeezing through broken slats in the fence to our allotment, then skirting the adjacent Polytechnic playing field.

'Are they really digging a tunnel?' I asked Nigel. 'Like the prisoners-of-war did?'

'Of course. We're going under the fence.' And he picked up some pieces of wood, scattered across the ground floor of the bombed house, and started back.

David and George sawed the wood into suitable lengths for props, then hammered them in position to make a wooden frame at the start of the tunnel. 'We'll have to shore it up all the way,' they agreed.

Tunnelling took several days — and many more planks of wood. Sometimes thick roots from the large old oak in the allotment had to be sawn through, as inch-by-inch the narrow tunnel edged the short distance to the fence, and the Deightons' garden next-door. I was allowed down the hole once, to slither into the darkness with a flickering candle, but I soon wriggled out again.

'We must be there by now,' George was saying. 'Let's measure.'

'A bit further,' said David.

Eventually, satisfied they had passed under the fence, David jumped into the hole. 'Time to break through,' he said, squeezing into the tunnel, and I watched his legs disappearing.

On a patch of well-dug soil next door, tiny grains of earth started to move as the point of a thin stick slowly appeared.

'You're through!' shouted Nigel. At the same time I saw Mother coming down the garden.

'What does Mrs Deighton mean about a tunnel?' she queried, staring at the hole in the ground. Then looking up, she noticed the stick waving out of the soil in our elderly neighbours' vegetable plot. A look of horror spread over her face.

Reluctantly our dangerous tunnelling exploits had to end, and all that remained was a partly in-filled tunnel and a mound of earth in the corner of the garden.

Next morning I saw David staring at the rough triangular area again, and I went to see what he was looking at.

'I want bricks from the bombed house,' he said, decisively. 'And tiles as well.'

'What are you going to do?'

'You'll see.'

Nigel and I carried the bricks back one or two at a time, but David always wanted more. No one seemed to see us as we pushed through the hedge into the garden of the bomb-damaged house, so the pile of bricks grew. David, meanwhile, cleared a level space by the tall wooden slatted fence between our garden and the allotment.

Over the next few days, I watched as two narrow walls, neatly constructed with Father's cement, began to take shape. They jutted out from the fence, with a third wall joining the other two together. This one had a narrow doorway in the centre for a tiny wooden door.

'I'll need more tiles than that,' David said. So Nigel and I went off to get them.

When we returned, David had nailed wooden slats across the top of the brickwork to support a roof, and he was starting to fix the tiles. He ended with the last row of tiles attached to the top of the fence. The little house looked extremely professional to me, but David's masterpiece was the chimney, connected to an authentic looking fireplace. With the metal chimney pipe firmly in place, we collected paper, wood and a few pieces of precious coal, then kneeling in the doorway David carefully lit the fire. He shut the tiny door and we stood back, watching as the first faint trickle of smoke appeared from the chimney.

'It works! It really works!' And we ran back across the garden to get our mother to come and see it.

As we stood on the concrete path outside the kitchen, watching the smoke curling into the sky, the trickle became thicker. Thin wisps were escaping from cracks around the door. Something was wrong. Grabbing buckets of water we rushed to the little house as smoke poured out. Sadly we realised that David's only mistake had been to build a wooden fireplace against the wooden fence!

'At least we can use the hole in the fence to get into the allotment and the field, ' said David, practically. 'It's much bigger than the other hole.'

Something woke me one dark night, and peering into the shadowy bedroom I searched for 'things' that I was convinced were waiting to pounce. I listened acutely, not for planes and guns now but for a possible step on the stairs or the creak of the landing floorboards. I didn't move; I couldn't; because with the slightest discernible movement the unseen 'things' would leap out at me.

Breathing shallowly I stared into the darkness, picking out the bulky shapes of dressing table and wardrobe; searching for anything unfamiliar. When my heart had steadied, I inched imperceptibly into a different position, first one foot, then the other, until I could spring up and grab the light pull above my head.

The 'things' immediately disappeared, although I was sure they still lurked outside on the landing. But having put on the light, if I eventually turned it off I would be plunged momentarily into inky blackness far worse than before. So although I knew I was wasting precious electricity, I left the light on, as I listened to the reassuring quarter chimes of the grandfather clock, until I drifted back to sleep.

Some nights when I woke, despite the 'writhing snakes' waiting to twist round my bare legs, I hurried to my parents' room. If Mother was awake I slipped in beside her. But if she was asleep I stood by the bed not wanting to disturb her, yet hoping she would wake and see me. When I was too cold to go on standing there, I crept silently back to my own bed.

One moonlit night, after preliminary peerings, my eyes picked out the reflection of a ladder on the wall. The curtains were open and I could clearly see the shadow of the rungs. Someone was trying to get in. Easing myself quietly out of bed, I made for the open door and my parents' bedroom to warn them.

'It's the moon,' said Mother patiently, as she went to investigate. 'It's reflecting the pattern of the window on the wall.'

I was only partly convinced, but she showed me how it was impossible to put a ladder up to my window because of the angle of the porch roof below. Then one night we really did have a burglar, but I didn't hear about it until the next morning.

'There was great excitement in the night!' Father said, as we all converged on the kitchen for breakfast. 'Mummy and I heard rustling noises coming from the hall, so I slipped out of bed and went to the landing.'

We were used to the way he prolonged his stories for maximum effect, and waited, wondering what he was going to say.

'The sounds were louder now,' he carried on, 'and as I started down the stairs a figure scuttled out from the understairs cupboard.'

'Did you get him?' said Nigel.

'A *burglar?*'

Father continued, 'I charged down the stairs and through the hall, but he had a head start, so by the time I ran into the garden he had gone.'

'How did he get in?'

'Did he *steal* anything?'

We were all talking at once.

'He must have climbed up to the fanlight above the door, and put his hand through to open the kitchen window. Then he unlocked the door when he was inside.'

'We must make sure the fanlight's always closed,' said Mother.

'That's how I get in,' Nigel admitted. 'When the door's locked.'

'Did he *steal* anything?' I said again, wondering what he might have taken.

'Luckily he dropped our bank books and war bonds as he ran through the kitchen,' said Father. 'I phoned the police . . .'

'And that's the funny part,' interrupted Mother.

But Father persisted, 'A policeman arrived from West Dulwich Police Station and said he hadn't seen anything suspicious on his way over.'

'What did he expect to see?' said David.

'He said he only passed a man in a white raincoat.'

'And my long white Dannimac is the only thing that was stolen!' Mother finished.

After that incident I viewed the understairs cupboard with suspicion. Even so, when Janet and her parents came to see us — her first visit since she stayed with us in Swansea — Nigel and I showed her our 'lift' that went down to the cupboard from the wardrobe in my bedroom. Janet and I climbed inside, squatting down with our knees up under our chins, while Nigel closed the door. In the darkness we felt the 'lift' starting to rattle its way down, as we rocked against the sides. Outside, Nigel pushed the wardrobe to and fro.

'I'll meet you downstairs,' we heard him call, his voice getting quieter as we supposedly descended.

Crouching in total blackness, Janet and I heard distant footsteps stomping on the stairs, then knocking and banging on the door as Nigel tried to open it. But it appeared to be stuck fast. We could hear him rattling the door handle outside.

'The door's jammed,' he shouted through to us. 'It won't open. I'll have to send you back up again.'

With more rattling and rocking, I assured Janet that we could get out in my bedroom. When the 'lift' stopped, Nigel opened the door with ease and out we climbed. Janet believed us, of course.

'Bananas at Bartletts!' The news flashed round the village as a lengthening queue trailed away from the local greengrocers, and as soon as she could, Mother left the bookshop to join the queue.

'We can have bananas for pudding,' she said later that day, handing round the rare treat.

I carefully peeled back the skin and ate with delight. I even scraped my teeth down the inside of the bitter yellow strips, before popping the final piece of banana into my mouth.

'Do you think they've got bananas in Brixton?' I said. 'Can we see tomorrow when we go shopping?'

But there were no bananas by the time Mother and I reached Brixton Market. So with our shopping completed, we caught a bus back to Herne Hill, then trudged up Burbage Road. Nigel wandered into the kitchen as we emptied our packages on the table.

'There was a strange woman with a foreign accent,' he said. 'She asked to see "Leelee". But I said you were out.'

Mother looked annoyed. 'That sounds like that *wretched* Hella,' she said. 'She must have been released from prison. Why did she come here?'

'I don't know.'

'How did she know our address? What did she *want?*'

'She didn't say. She just asked for you,' said Nigel, defensively.

'Now I suppose she'll go and see Uncle Ern. Did she ask about him?'

Mother's Uncle Ernest — Grandpa's younger brother — lived in Beckenham. He wasn't on the phone and Mother seldom saw him, but she felt she must warn him about Hella. I went with her, hurrying up Burbage Road to catch a train from West Dulwich to Kent House Station. From here we walked the short distance to Barnmead Road, and all the while Mother worried over what Hella wanted and whether she was going to pester us now she had been released from Holloway.

Auntie Jessie opened the door and was thrilled to see us. She made a great fuss of me, before taking us into the small neat sitting room where Uncle Ern was reading the paper. As we went into the room he jumped up to greet us. And I burst into tears. For there, as far as I was concerned, was Grandpa. I hardly knew or even remembered seeing Uncle Ern before. He even spoke like Grandpa and his mannerisms were just the same. I cried and cried and could not be consoled.

But we heard no more from Hella.

Now the war was over, Nigel and I were allowed to cycle further afield. Some Saturdays after lunch we pedalled along the almost traffic-free roads to Champion Hill. Here, we leant our bikes against the railings and went through the '6d boys' turnstile, to watch Dulwich Hamlet, our local football team, in a home match. When Auntie Gladys stayed for the weekend she came too, and not only paid our sixpences but shouted and cheered for Dulwich Hamlet as enthusiastically as we did.

Occasionally Nigel and I cycled to Selhurst Park for a more important game of football by Crystal Palace, our nearest Third Division South team. But that cost more money, so when we were short there was only one thing to do.

Before the day of the match, we set off on our bikes up College Road, past the little toll house and toll gate, on past Sydenham Hill Station to Crystal Palace, then down the steep hill to Beckenham. We found our way to Barnmead Road to see Uncle Ern and Auntie Jessie, who were always delighted to see us on these infrequent visits. We usually stayed for an excellent tea, but when we said good-bye, we knew Uncle Ern would press a shilling into our hands. At that moment our visit to Crystal Palace was assured.

'You haven't said, "Honestly truly *doobs*",' I said to Nigel one Saturday, when we were in the garden trying to unravel the whereabouts of a mysterious spy.

'I don't need to; you know I couldn't make the whole thing up.'

I had a vague suspicion that Nigel had something to do with our stumbling across that first chance clue, mainly because he avoided making our agreed declaration of honesty. Adding our specially invented word 'doobs' had been David's idea many months earlier, so we would know, without any doubt, that what we told each other was the absolute truth. But this time Nigel hadn't said it.

We found the second suspicious clue, with his prompting, when we happened upon a pear lying in the fountain at the top of Burbage Road, and Nigel bit into it.

'You can't eat it,' I said. 'It might be poisoned!' After all Mother had told us about not picking things up, here was Nigel biting into a discarded pear.

'Of course it's not . . . Uhh, what's this?' And from the centre of the pear he pulled out a small piece of paper. Hidden inside was a strange looking coin. 'It's a German pfennig and a message,' Nigel added, in mock surprise.

I only half suspected Nigel had planted it. After all, I reasoned, how could he get a German coin? But as the trail moved on, and more bizarre coincidences emerged, I began to have serious doubts.

The final clue led us, one quiet Sunday afternoon, to St Leonard's Church in Thurlow Park Road. By now we were hard on the heels of the spy, and although part of me suspected Nigel, I was still worried that we were getting too involved. We propped our

Toll House and Toll Gate, Dulwich

The drinking fountain, Dulwich Village

bikes by the kerb before moving cautiously over the rubble around the war-damaged building. Nigel was behind me when I heard a sudden clatter. I spun round as he jumped back against the scaffolding covering the church.

'Did you see that?' he said in a theatrical whisper, stooping down to pick up a broken slate. 'There's someone on the roof throwing tiles at us!'

I stared in amazement.

'Look! Up there!' he hissed. 'Too late, he's ducked down.'

I became increasingly suspicious as we moved round the church and it was only Nigel who saw him. 'I don't believe there really is a spy,' I said at last. 'Say, "Honestly truly doobs I've got nothing to do with it!" or I won't believe you.'

But Nigel wouldn't.

'It was Norman and Henry Bones, that's where you got the idea from,' I said, knowing Nigel liked the boy detectives on *Children's Hour* just as much as I did.

'No I didn't.'

'Yes you did. It's the sort of thing they do.'

In the end, after further argument, Nigel related how he had thought up the idea for his elaborate hoax.

By now, my bedroom, at 1 Landing Way, had become the head office for all the 'M.G.' commercial and social establishments in Devizes — the needlework shop; stamp shop; printing press; library; nature and animal society; gardening store; the League for Others (under M.G. supervision); the Helpers Club; the Invalid Association; and the Birthday Club.

I was inspired to start the League for Others during the autumn term, because of a charitable trust called the Ranyard Mission I heard about at school. We were asked to donate some of our toys to be distributed to poor children in London through the Mission, and after two senior girls had delivered the toys to Ranyard Mission House, I listened to their graphic account.

The scheme struck a chord with me; perhaps I could buy toys and distribute them in Devizes? To raise the money, I hung a 'stocking' on my bedroom door, with a notice saying: *The League for Others*. I was pleased when I saw my parents drop in the odd coin from time to time, and David said he put in a halfpenny or farthing he found.

But when I emptied the stocking there were buttons, paper clips, nails and old stamps, too. With little cash collected to buy toys, I covered spice containers with coloured paper for 'useful pots', crayoned circles of cardboard and threaded string through each centre as 'whizzers', and made similar unlikely 'toys'.

'Who are they for?' asked David, seeing me busily cutting out tiny net Christmas stockings and carefully stitching them round in red wool. Then I realised 'the poor' of Devizes were us!

'Why don't you buy a few more toys from Woolworths,' Mother said tactfully, knowing how much time I had spent on the project, 'and give the stockings to children in King's College Hospital?'

'I could get Mary Marsh to help,' I said, enthusiastically, and my spirits rose again.

So when Christmas approached, Mary and I proudly boarded a bus at Herne Hill to take six tiny Christmas stockings to the children's ward at the hospital. I was so pleased, I left the collecting stocking on the door handle of 1 Landing Way, ready for the following year.

That first peaceful Christmas, Nigel and I raced down Croxted Road and along Norwood Road to Herne Hill. We heard a tram rattling along behind us, so we jumped off our bikes where the tram lines converged close to the kerb. We always laughed when we saw the warning sign 'TRAM PINCH', and wondered who did the pinching.

Once the tram had clanked slowly by, we cycled on along Railton Road to Brixton. Leaving our bikes by the kerb, we looked in the brightly decorated shop windows, before weaving our way through Christmas shoppers to the street market behind the station.

M. G. LT. D.

1, LANDING WAY
or
107, BURBAGE ROAD.

THE M.G. NEEDLEWORK SHOP.
THE M.G. STAMP SHOP
THE M.G. PRINTING PRESS
THE M.G. LIBRARY
THE M.G. NATURE & ANIMAL SOCIETY
THE M. G. GARDENING STORE
THE LEAGUE FOR OTHERS (UNDER M.G. SUPERVISION)
THE HELPERS CLUB
THE INVALID ASSOCIATION
THE BIRTHDAY CLUB.

THESE ARE ALL BRANCHES OF THE M.G. GENERAL STORE.

(PLEASE TURN OVER)

The M.G. Enterprises

Here, a huge orange mound caught our attention as it spilled out over one of the stalls.

'Tangerines!' we said together, surprised by the unbelievable sight.

'Threepence a pound. Let's get some.'

We queued up for a pound of tangerines and ate them between us. Eating in the street was definitely not allowed, but as I wasn't wearing school uniform I knew no one could report me. Next we made for Woolworths, where we wandered around choosing inexpensive gifts from our Christmas present lists.

Back at home, I rummaged through our bag of ancient wrapping paper and carefully wrapped my presents in the flattened pieces, saved each year. I was immersed in the magic of Christmas, which stood out like a shining beacon through the long dark winter. It wasn't just the presents, for they were inexpensive and often homemade. It was the whole wonderful event; the amazing Christmas story; the feeling of excitement; singing carols from door to door with no threat of bombs or raids.

Nigel and I painted and crayoned strips of paper for paper-chains, which we stuck together in loops with a glutinous mixture made from flour and water, hoping the paste would hold. Then we lavishly decorated the playroom and our bedrooms, draping the paper chains from the centre light out to the walls with happy abandon. We climbed on chairs to festoon sprays of holly behind pictures, along the picture rails and on any available surface.

David and our parents decorated the hall and dining room more artistically with holly and ivy, even trailing it through the bannisters and up the stairs. And I made tiny bells by pressing silver milk tops over a thimble to create the shapes, and carefully sewing a loop of cotton through each one to hang it from the greenery. Precious pieces of pre-war tinsel added an authentic touch, and for me the house was transformed into an enchanting wonderland.

About a week before Christmas, we had collected the holly and ivy from the woods beyond the Polytechnic playing field. We always said 'the woods', but it was really just a small triangle of rough bushes and sparse trees; a piece of no-man's land tapering off between disused tennis courts and two cricket fields bordering Gallery Road. Sometimes we had logging expeditions in the woods, when we gathered up dead branches to cut up and burn on the playroom fire. And at Christmas, fires blazed in the hall and dining room, too.

Sitting close to the playroom fire, with one side of me roasting while the other side stayed cold, I made my Christmas cards and present tags from old pictures. And this year I struggled to make an elaborately decorated 'festive hat' for the competition Mother had organised for our Boxing Day party. In the weeks before Christmas I had seen special food being spirited away in tins and hidden in strange places. Then on Christmas Eve I helped display it on the three-tiered cake stand in the dining room. But I knew that not a nut not a date, not one single thing could be eaten before the party.

Purring loudly Fluff licked my face, waking me early on Christmas morning. He pushed his way under the bedclothes and while he settled in the warm patch where I had been lying, I stretched out to reach the knobbly sock lying at the foot of my bed. I felt down the body of the sock first, hoping there would be a dress-the-doll cut-out book. Then I switched on the light and, burrowing under the blankets to keep warm, started opening the small presents.

Sounds of rustling paper from the boys' rooms told me they were also undoing parcels and eating sweets bought with our parents' coupons, while downstairs our main presents waited in the dining room for the afternoon. But before this longed-for moment there would be church with the whole family, and then the Christmas dinner to prepare.

As soon as we returned from church, and the smell of roast pork and apple sauce filled the house, I busied myself laying the playroom table, and helped to carry hot dishes of home-grown vegetables from the kitchen. Now we were ready to put on our 'festive hats', as Father carved and the meal progressed.

The best part, I thought, was when the Christmas pudding appeared, sprinkled with castor sugar to look like frost and with a sprig of red-berried holly on top. I had watched Mother making the pudding several weeks beforehand and saw her pushing sixpences and silver threepenny pieces inside.

Cracker pulling came next. We had made our own crackers from crêpe paper, with mottoes, small gifts and rolled-up hats saved from pre-war years. Finally, with surprising speed, we cleared the table and set to on the washing up. This had to be finished before 3 o'clock, to be ready in the dining room for the King's speech.

My mind wandered off the speech as I surveyed the mound of presents in their familiar second-hand wrappings spilling over the floor. I glimpsed a 'To Margaret' label and tried to guess what was inside the package. Was there an Enid Blyton adventure? Or a small parcel that might be an Observer's book or a Nelson's Classic, in the series I was collecting? And was that the shape of a Rupert annual for Nigel? If so I could read it too.

A roll of drums on the wireless, announcing the National Anthem, told me the speech had ended, so I stood to attention with the others. Now, at last, we pulled up our chairs or sat on the floor round the central pile of irregular shaped parcels.

'To David, a very happy Christmas with love from Auntie Gladys,' Father read out.

Whatever size the present, he took each one in turn, read out the label and handed the parcel to the recipient. We all watched as awkward knots were untied and the paper carefully removed and placed in a 'good pile' or in the 'rubbish box'.

'To Mummy, love from Margaret,' I heard, when David's present had been revealed.

'I know who this one's from.' said Nigel, picking up a parcel from the pile. 'It smells of mothballs!'

'Put it back, Nigel. I'm not ready for that one yet.' And Father carried on.

We had found out that the aunts had a large drawer, where they collected presents bought from sales-of-work or acquired during the year. They liberally scattered mothballs amongst the handmade woollen gifts, and the strong smell invaded the entire contents — even bars of chocolate. But chocolate was chocolate to us, however strange the taste.

I knew we would have to write 'thank-you letters' afterwards, so I scribbled down the details as our elaborate ceremony continued to the final parcel.

Now, still sitting in our circle for cups of tea and home-made Christmas cake, I examined the presents: 1946 diary, hand-knitted jumper, colouring book with pencils, lead farm animals, the polished wood book-ends Nigel had made for me at school, and cherished books to add to my 'library'. I had grown used to this annual ritual and wouldn't have wanted it any other way. So with a warm feeling of satisfaction, I carried my presents upstairs to find them a place in my bedroom.

We were up early on Boxing Day to prepare for the family party: moving chairs, making ready the 'stage' for our entertainment, sharpening pencils for 'parlour games' and tidying the house before our snack lunch of Christmas leftovers.

Carrying their festive hats, Grandma and the aunts arrived first, punctually as usual, and accompanied by Grandma's sisters, Mary and Edith. Great-Aunt Mary, or Auntie Polly as she was affectionately called, was the sweetest little old lady. In her quiet, genteel way she had told me stories of the days when she was art mistress at Malvern Girls' College, but now she lived with her youngest sister, Edith, in Ovingdean in Sussex.

Unpredictable Edith, also an artist, had changed the pronunciation of her name in a variety of ways, finally settling on Ed-ith-a. Being eccentric, as we thought, she never surprised us by the things she did or the presents she gave.

'Thank you, Aunt Editha,' said Nigel, politely, opening his small present. But to David he mouthed, 'What is it?'

'A gas mask strap!' laughed David.

Auntie Gladys, off-duty from her hospital, and Mrs Mac and Stuart crowded into the hall with the others, sitting near the log fire on chairs we had lined up in rows of two or three. A curtain, temporarily hanging from a pole from picture rail to picture rail, now closed off the stage area between the porch and the playroom.

Buoyed up with excitement, I peeped through the curtain, watching the audience reading the official programmes David had typed for the 'Greenaways' entertainment.

'Hushes' and settling-down sounds came from the hall as Father pulled back the curtain and David, Nigel and I faced the audience. I didn't mind standing there with the boys, while Mother in the playroom accompanied us on the piano. We counted the opening bars, then started our prolonged rendering of 'Come to the Fair'. But after Stuart had waded through his recitation of 'John Gilpin', I sang 'Early One Morning', which was far more embarrassing.

More songs and recitations followed, leading to the interval, when the grown-ups played the piano, sang and recited, while in the hall David, Nigel and I prepared the stage for our short sketch. For several weeks we had practised and rehearsed, although Mother had initially chivvied us into taking part and had helped, painstakingly, with the authentic costumes and scenery. But once the audience had trooped back to the hall, the sketch seemed to flash by as our entertainment came to an end. The opening notes of 'God Save the King' came from the playroom, and we all stood to attention.

Scenery and props were hastily cleared away, while cakes, tea and plates of Father's special sandwiches were carried into the dining room, where the dates and nuts could at last be eaten. To round off the party, after the festive hat competition, we divided into two teams for acting games and my favourite drawing game.

'Right now, one team in the playroom, the other team in the dining room,' said Father, relishing his usual job of organising. 'Ready everyone?' He stood by the hall fire as a member from each team hurried out to be told the first object on his previously prepared list.

In front of the dining room fire, we crowded round the card table as Auntie Flo started to draw.

'A hippopotamus?'

'Mmm.' More lines were added.

'Over eating?'

'Christmas?'

'Mmm.' More drawing.

'Jonah and the whale.' said somebody.

'Yes, dears,' said Auntie Flo at last.

As soon as the object was guessed, another member dashed out for the next item, until one team finished the list.

I was glad Christmas was on a Thursday that year, because when it came at the weekends there were extra church services to go to, so our parlour games had to be curtailed.

'I hate going to St Barnabas,' said Nigel, one cold February Sunday, when we returned from morning service.

'So do I,' I said. 'But we've got to go.'

'I don't see why. We could go somewhere else.'

'Where?'

'St Paul's on Herne Hill.'

'Daddy will never let us.'

'I'm going to ask him,' said Nigel, boldly.

Father went to church every Sunday without fail. I knew it was important to him, because during Lent and on Good Fridays he wore his 'Good Friday face' like a sombre mask. I was always glad when he transformed into happiness on Easter Sundays.

One Sunday he had decided that David, Nigel and I were 'lacking in religious instruction', so he had started giving us formal Sunday school lessons at home. He read and discussed passages from the huge family Bible, but we fidgeted with embarrassment and eventually Nigel and I had agreed to go with him to St Barnabas instead.

The three of us cycled to the massive, cold church on the brow of Calton Avenue, where we joined Grandma and the aunts. For Nigel and me this meant extra best behaviour, as we sat through the long service, and sometimes I felt faint and had to be taken outside.

'It's not such a high service at St Paul's,' we pleaded, when Nigel asked if we could go there instead. And we were relieved when Father said we could.

David was allowed to stay at home and help Mother with the dinner, while Nigel and I cycled off to church. I liked watching Mr Dyer, the vicar of St Paul's, waving his arms about during his flamboyant sermons. It was far more fun than St Barnabas. We renamed him 'Dig-a-well-Dyer' after his lively, forthright address coercing the congregation to go out and dig a well, although I wasn't sure where we had to dig it.

Once we met Stuart after the service and whizzing down Herne Hill on the pavement — the three of us on Nigel's bike — we were stopped by a policeman. He took our names and addresses and we were terrified he would tell our parents. But luckily we heard no more.

Each Sunday, when we returned home from church, we smelt delicious roast meat, and saw vegetables piled up waiting to be cooked. It was our job to lay the playroom table and I usually stirred the gravy too. When we had roast lamb, I collected sprigs of mint from the garden and chopped them finely for mint sauce, while David finished preparing the pudding.

'Where's David?' Nigel said, one Sunday. 'Hasn't he made one of his 4321 puddings?'

'He's doing his homework this morning,' Mother explained.

'What're we having then?'

'Wait-and-see pudding!' Mother always said that when she hadn't decided.

'I'll make it today,' said Nigel, to everyone's surprise. 'It's going to be *different*.' And he shut himself in the kitchen to prepare it. But when he proudly produced his sponge-like 4321 pudding — the name giving the proportions of ingredients — the only difference between his and David's, was that Nigel had added an overdose of bright green colouring.

Nigel and I occasionally did our own 'cooking'. We could never eke out our meagre sweet ration, even 2-ounces of dolly mixture didn't go far, and off-ration fruit bars from the grocers cost more money. Instead we raided the larder and usually mixed up strange concoctions of sugar, cocoa and syrup.

One afternoon, at the end of the Easter holidays, I went into the kitchen as Nigel hastily cleared away evidence of his 'cooking'. 'I've made some ice cream,' he said.

'Ice cream?'

'Yes, you can try it.'

I dipped my finger in the semi-frozen, off-white mixture. It was lumpy and tasted strongly of sugary vanilla. 'Mmm, it's good. Bags scrape!'

'You can't say that when *I'm* cooking,' he said, indignantly.

'Mummy lets me!'

'That's different.'

When Mother was cooking I shouted 'bags scrape' as fast as I could, otherwise instead of scraping the mixing bowl I only had a spoon or fork to lick.

'Why can't I have. . .' I began, but David interrupted me.

'If you don't hurry up we can't go,' he said, coming into the kitchen, closely followed by Stuart.

'What's that?' Stuart eyed the bowl of mixture, quizzically.

But David had promised to take us out in a rowing boat on Dulwich Park pond and he was impatient to go. So Nigel divided his ice cream into four equal shares and hurriedly scraped the last clinging particles from the bowl.

We finished our ice cream and set off on our bikes for the boating lake. But hardy had the boat started dipping through the water, than we hurried back to the landing stage. Feeling increasingly ill we cycled home, and I crawled into bed with the large, white, china chamber pot conveniently near.

'Whatever have you been eating?' asked Mother, as one by one we were violently sick.

'Ice cream,' Nigel reluctantly admitted. But he had to agree that raw semolina wasn't the best ingredient, and I wondered what else he had put in it.

Back at school I told my friends what had happened. 'You can have the recipe,' I said. 'It *really* works. You can miss the gym competition then.'

'Oh yes? What about those Plasticine toffees you made last term?' countered Mary Marsh.

I wasn't really surprised no one wanted to hear about the sick-mixture, after all my Plasticine toffees, liberally sprinkled with peppermint essence and wrapped in used toffee papers, had been realistic. And however much I hated parading round in my brown school knickers for the annual gym competition, I couldn't face being sick again to justify missing it.

When the dreaded competition loomed near, I sat on the garage floor with a sharp stone, repeatedly hitting my knee. The previous year, when I was being chased, my leg had skidded along the gravel so a large bandage had meant no gym competition. But this year although I tried to make a cut, unexpected reflexes stopped me from hitting hard enough. I was annoyed when I only had a bruise and no bandage to exclude me from the competition.

What I most disliked was being watched. But Miss Buzzard, our prim, aging gym mistress, watched each one of us as we walked along a narrow bar. It started at floor level and was gradually raised to greater heights, while Miss Buzzard called out in her quiet, clipped voice:

'Head up, shoulders back, tummy in, tail down.'

This ordeal was to gain a 'posture stripe'. So week by week I had persevered under Miss Buzzard's careful scrutiny, until I confidently pinned a gilt-edged, maroon badge to my tunic.

But school was only a temporary diversion, because Devizes, our all-consuming make-believe world, had become my main preoccupation. And Devizes demanded more and more time.

120

Map of Devizes

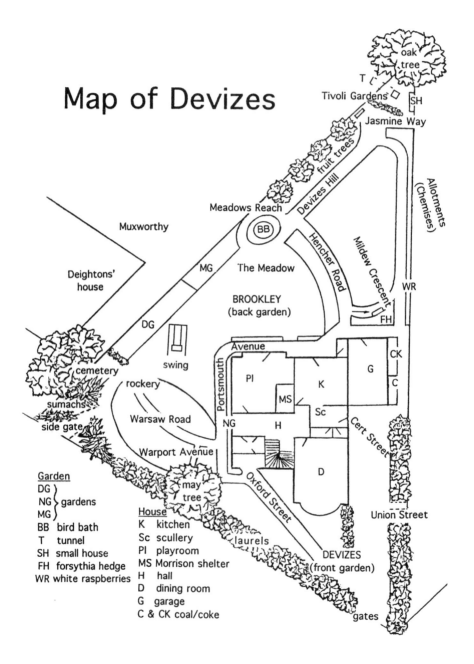

Garden
DG ⎫
NG ⎬ gardens
MG ⎭
BB bird bath
T   tunnel
SH small house
FH forsythia hedge
WR white raspberries

House
K   kitchen
Sc scullery
Pl playroom
MS Morrison shelter
H   hall
D   dining room
G   garage
C & CK coal/coke

9. Always Devizes: 1946

I saw Rosemary and Ann Crews peering over the fence by the sumachs, when I was crawling out of the hidey-hole under the laurel bushes. This was where the Tune family lived in Devizes. Kenneth Butterfield was driving along Warsaw Road and didn't see Rosemary and Ann at first.

'Can we play?' they called out, and opened the side gate into the garden.

'We're not *playing*,' said Nigel brusquely, hurrying away in the person of Kenneth Butterfield towards Hencher Road.

'What are you doing then?'

'It's Devizes.'

'We can play Devizes. What do we have to do?' They had followed him to Hencher Road, then wandered into Mildew Crescent.

'Well for a start you can't go the wrong way down Mildew Crescent. It's a one-way street.'

'It doesn't say it's a one-way street.'

'Well it is.'

'All right, so what do we have to do now?'

'They haven't said wodge yet,' I joined in.

'Wodge! What does that mean?'

'You say *wodge* to show you're in Devizes. When you're not in Devizes you say *unwodge*,' Nigel reluctantly explained.

Rosemary and Ann stared at us in disbelief. 'Go on. What else?'

'If you haven't got a car you have to go along the roads like this,' I said, walking slowly, heel touching toe, one foot in front of the other.

'If you've got a car you can walk normally,' said Nigel.

'Alfred Fangster's got to limp everywhere. But if he gets a lift he can walk behind the driver at normal speed.'

'Can't anyone run?'

'Only fire engines and police cars.'

'And ambulances,' I added.

They watched in silence as Nigel drove away along Portsmouth Avenue, with much changing of gear.

'Why's he got that paint tin lid?'

'That's his *car*.' I was amazed they didn't realise. 'Big lids are big cars and little lids are little cars.' It seemed obvious to me.

Rosemary and Ann tried to fit in to Devizes, but they didn't have our complete dedication, and our unwritten rules were too complex to explain to them. After a while Ann said, 'Let's play something else now.'

Nigel and I were shocked. No on *plays* Devizes we told them. So they soon left to find something else to do.

Meanwhile, David, with great enthusiasm, had rigged up an elaborate 'car' using a frame of wood held up by straps over his shoulders. But the unwieldy contraption took too much space to park on the narrow 'roads', compared with a simple steering wheel lid. Traffic lights from Hencher Road to Portsmouth Avenue were another of David's inventions. But they involved manually changing three torches, so they had a short life.

Despite the abundance of cars in Devizes, if I heard a real car engine I dashed to the front gate to scribble down the number in a home-made notebook, for we seldom saw private cars in these early postwar days.

'Devizes Borough Council's been asked to clear dried grass from the Meadow,' announced Horace Dixon, Chief Clerk to the Highways Department, reading a letter from Mrs Lilian Green. 'I'm sending a gang of men with utility vans.'

So we filled old galvanised buckets and we cleared the weeds from Devizes Hill, too. But to the 'gang of men' it was serious work; we weren't just filling buckets, we were council workers loading our vans. And Mother became adept at getting odd jobs done in the garden, with the willing help of Devizes characters.

I was so involved with the job in hand that I lost my little round glasses somewhere in the garden, and although we searched meticulously they couldn't be found. To our surprise, when Mother took me to have my eyes tested for a new pair, I no longer needed to wear them. 'Let the fresh air get to her eyes. It will do far more good,' we were told.

I was like a new person.

'WHERE ARE MY CLOTHES?' I shouted at David one morning.

'I know you've hidden them.'

'Why should I hide them?' he said, evasively, as he dressed for school.

'Where are they?' I turned my bedroom upside down, but there were no clothes, and I couldn't convince Mother that David had taken them. Eventually, when I made my bed, I found the lost clothes where David had hidden them between the blankets. But now I was late for breakfast and afterwards I had to run down Burbage Road, for I was late for school, too.

I knew the doors leading to the lower cloakroom would be locked promptly at 9 o'clock, but as I jumped off the bus and hurried up Trinity Rise, I hoped a kind fifth-former might let me in through their cloakroom. But I was out of luck, and with the sinking realisation that I really was late, I made my way up the side path to the front entrance.

I climbed the wide, stone steps under a pillared canopy to the imposing front door and rang the bell. The echoes resounded inside and I waited for the elderly school secretary to open the door.

'Late, Margaret? Go and sit on the bench.' And under her disapproving gaze I walked across the entrance hall and sat on the polished bench outside the headmistress's study.

Sitting in silence, I looked up at the impressive domed roof of this inner hallway and down at the tiled floor, studying the patterns. I could hear muffled sounds of the school getting ready for prayers; distant footsteps; a closing door. The waiting was far worse than the regal appearance of Miss Gordon Ewen, for she smiled her generous smile, heard my faltering excuse and asked me to try to be more punctual. That was all. But I knew I would be marked late in the register and on my end of term report.

I often ran breathlessly up Trinity Rise after that; on past the netball courts, with no one running with me to squeeze in before the doors were locked, or to share the intimidating ordeal of being late. But I couldn't be downcast for long. I had important Devizes activities to look forward to, which were always waiting for me at home.

Busily working in my bedroom — at 1 Landing Way — I could hear Nigel, equally involved with the N.A. Stores and all his other 'N.A.' enterprises at 3A Landing Way. Nigel also made tiny Devizes bank notes from special pink paper and issued them through Owen's Paper Store. He assured us he couldn't make his own private hoard of bank notes, because the paper was in short supply, but I wasn't entirely convinced.

We sold or swapped anything, within the family, from pin cushions to paper weights; book-ends to garden plants; and any number of second-hand goods. David produced and distributed leaflets announcing the services of a professional artist. The artist, Robert J. Hobbs, at 26 Devizes Hill (phone Brookley 3610) also offered to illustrate books, hoping they would be published by Burbage Publications at 9 Landing Way.

When Burbage Publications had the use of an ancient typewriter, my M.G. Press suffered a drop in orders. To compensate for this shortfall, I produced an assortment of tiny puzzle books, each containing a selection of jumbled letters, spot-the-difference pictures and similar puzzles.

But paper was a problem. So short of supplies were we, that I tore the fly leaves and end papers from some of my books. After all, I questioned, why should books have plain pieces of paper front and back when they weren't needed? Despite this maltreatment, I valued my books and with the help of my John Bull printing set, numbered and stamped each one with 'M.G. LIBRARY'.

Even with the acute shortage of paper, Owen's Paper Store and both the 'printing presses' managed to produce a vast quantity of tiny stationery — advertising leaflets, advice notes, compliments

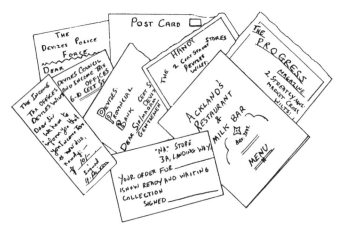

A vast quantity of tiny stationery

slips, order forms, headed notepaper and just about anything needed by our Devizes characters and businesses. With 'one-sided' paper Father gave us, we made miniature packets of two-inch square envelopes. The interiors were variously decorated with typing or printing, depending on the one-sided paper available.

One Saturday morning, when I was busily writing in my room, I heard someone lift the flap of the gate-legged table on the landing. I looked round my door as David set out a ruler, a thin stick, a small brass cog-wheel from an old clock and some sheets of gummed paper covered with neat rows of identical tiny drawings.

'What are you doing?'

But he didn't answer, so I stood in the doorway watching, fascinated, as he put the stick through the cog-wheel then carefully rolled it over a piece of gummed paper.

'What's that for?'

'Perforations,' he said, without looking up.

To ensure the fine teeth in the cog-wheel perforated the paper, he lined up the sheet along the gap where the table-flap extended, then rolled the wheel first one way and then at right angles over the paper.

'What are you making?'

'Stamps, of course, for Devizes Post Office.'

'Margar. *Margaret,*' Mother's calling voice became more insistent, so I couldn't stop to watch, and ran downstairs to see what she wanted.

'There you are, Margar,' she said, as I went into the kitchen. 'Auntie Madge needs me in the shop this morning. Would you change Miss Avery's library books for me?'

Mother had taken this frail, elderly lady under her wing, but now I was increasingly taking over the library book routine and some of her shopping. On Saturday mornings I cycled to the bookshop to collect new library books, then on to the three-storey, Victorian house in Holmdean Avenue, where the old lady lived.

Miss Avery's landlady was never pleased at being disturbed, and made me feel I should definitely not be visiting. So I was glad when I found the front door had been left open and I could creep up the dingy staircase, unnoticed.

On the landing a pungent smell of stale air and decaying food became stronger, as I hesitated by the door to the small kitchen. I was half afraid I would find that Miss Avery had died during the night, but Mother had told me to knock loudly and call out before opening the bed-sitting room door. The same overpowering smell hung in the room, trapped by thick, dark curtains and heavy antique furniture. But I felt sorry for the frail old lady sitting in her upright chair, for she too seemed trapped.

When I could no longer postpone Miss Avery's frequent invitation to afternoon tea, I persuaded Nigel to come with me. We sat on the edge of our chairs in the claustrophobic room, making polite conversation. And all the while we wondered how to dispose of our rock-hard fruit cake, we suspected had been nibbled by mice.

ACKLAND'S RESTAURANT, GOOD FOOD, NICELY SERVED, FRIENDLY SERVICE, MODERATE RATES proclaimed the menu of Ackland's Restaurant and Milk Bar. Nigel had upgraded it from a snack bar, and Burbage publications had printed colourful headed notepaper and a folded card menu holder, with detachable menu affixed by four photograph corners.

'If you have any worries please see the Manager, Mr Michael Ackland,' the menu stated. But as it happened, Ackland's Restaurant seldom operated. The Rainbow Café, run by Mary Nottingham, was far more popular.

I never minded frequently getting our afternoon tea ready during the holidays. It was all part of Devizes. On Sundays, after church, I sometimes made tiny flans and pies from leftover pastry, and gradually progressed to making my own pastry and fairy cakes. Even so, The Rainbow Café more often served thick slices of bread with homemade jam or dripping — or just the loaf of bread for 'customers' to cut their own. And we took butter, margarine or jam sparingly from the packet or pot, without wastefully decanting it into dishes or leaving any on the side of our plates.

'Unwodge,' we would say, picking up the last crumbs with a licked finger. Then as fast as we could we shouted, 'Bags wash', 'Bags wipe' or 'Bags put'. Having divided up the washing up, another 'wodge' transformed us back to The Rainbow Café.

One afternoon, when David was out and Stuart was staying for tea, Nigel aimed the loaf of bread at Stuart and followed it by throwing the bread knife. Stuart ducked as the knife flew towards him. Amidst the shouting and clattering Mother hurried in to see the cause of the noise.

'Whatever's going on?' she demanded. And Nigel was sent to his bedroom to cool down.

But as soon as Mother left the room, Stuart and I, in earnest tones, discussed what had happened. Then we went out to the garden and threw clods of earth up to Nigel's window above the kitchen, to attract his attention.

'What d'you want?' Nigel said, leaning out.

'Lower your dressing gown cord down,' I whispered up to him. And standing on a kitchen chair I tied a hastily prepared bag of jam sandwiches to the cord for Nigel to haul up. Stuart and I had decided it wasn't fair for Nigel to be sent to his bedroom. After all, the argument had been part of Devizes.

'There's a concert at the Rainbow Café today,' I announced, one teatime, climbing on to the unlit stove in the corner of the kitchen. I stood with my head back, elbows raised and the tips of my outstretched fingers touching my non-existent cleavage, and started to sing, 'We'll gather lilacs in the spring again . . .'

Sometimes I sang 'Where e'er you Walk' or a song of my own making called 'Your Feet are my Feet and Always Mean to be'. Nigel told jokes and Stuart waded through 'John Gilpin'. But long before each performer could finish, the next turn started up. We were so busily involved with Devizes some days, I could hardly spare time to dash upstairs to the lavatory. I would wait and wait until I was almost bursting, then say, 'Unwodge' and charge up the edge of the stairs.

'Don't keep going up and down stairs, you'll wear the carpet

Nigel's bedroom above the kitchen

out,' Mother would sometimes call out. So we ran up the edge as often as we remembered.

Going up or coming down, I would leap over the stair just before the bend, as Nigel and I had done since we first saw the house. On that day we jumped over a mark on the bare board, and we continued our special ritual of jumping over the stair, even after it was covered with an aging carpet.

In the early days I had imagined there was a 'thing' upstairs waiting to pounce on me from the shadows, so someone was detailed to, 'Go upstairs with Margaret'. But when I had to go on my own, I crept quietly up to avoid disturbing the waiting menace. The bare, striped laths showing through the war-damaged ceilings added to the feeling that 'something' could be lurking up there, watching. I would hurry into my room, grab what I had gone for, then fly out again and down the stairs, banging the stairs' gate behind me and singing loudly as I leapt over the forbidden stair. My singing was to show I wasn't really afraid.

Sometimes I sang with gusto, 'When you're up to your neck in hot water, be like the kettle and sing!' Or I would sing Vera Lynn's sentimental wartime favourites, 'The White Cliffs of Dover' and 'We'll Meet Again', which I occasionally heard on *Housewives Choice.*

Hearing the signature tune of *Housewives Choice* at 9 o'clock on a weekday morning gave me a cosy, secure feeling. It usually meant I was tucked up in bed listening to the sounds coming up the stairs from the large, Bakelite wireless in the dining room. Just after 9 o'clock the wireless was turned down and I would hear Mother telephoning the school to say I was unwell. Now I could envisage a whole day of individual attention. By midday, often sneezing and streaming, I was downstairs huddled by the playroom fire, listening to Bill Gates introducing *Worker's Playtime* with another half hour of popular songs.

I always hated the days when I went down to breakfast and Mother wasn't there. 'Mummy's got a headache,' Father would say, and I knew it wasn't just a 'headache'; it was a migraine.

On these occasions we crept round the house talking in subdued voices, trying not to let doors bang in case she was asleep. At intervals through the day, a knock sounded on the floor above and someone would take up soda water to the darkened room, or empty the large white china chamber pot. And sometimes I hovered outside the bedroom door, wishing there was some way I could stop the constant sickness.

The frequency of her migraines meant she was often out of action. But my spirits rose as soon as she was up again, quickly resuming her normal busy life, for as well as helping in the aunts' bookshop, Mother sometimes taught at a nursery school in East Dulwich, or did voluntary work for the Care Committee of Dulwich Hamlet School. And she caught up with household jobs that had to be done, and news she had unwittingly missed.

I knew listening to the BBC News was still vital to my parents, and silence was essential before Alvar Lidell, Stuart Hibberd or Frank Phillips started to speak. Occasionally, after the midnight bulletin, I heard the big brown wireless striking up the National Anthem, and however sleepy I was I pulled myself out from my warm sheets to stand on my bed. Everyone stood for 'God Save the King', so I stood to attention until it was over.

But I wasn't really interested in the news. The wireless for me meant all the wonderful stories and plays on *Children's Hour* with Uncle Mac, and serials in the early evening. I would curl up in one of the big comfy armchairs in the dining room, hoping I wouldn't be disturbed.

The first notes of Wolf-Ferrari's 'Jewels of the Madonna', announcing *Ballet Shoes* — or 'Coronation Scot' heralding the Paul Temple series — were magical notes. With a thrill of antici-pation I was ready to hear the latest episode slowly unfold. *The Wind in the Willows* was another firm favourite, and I was in the meadow with Mole when he found himself rolling in the warm grass. I became immersed in Worzel Gummidge's strange life too.

One afternoon when David and Nigel went to see *Henry V*, I was disappointed when I couldn't go with them. But when they came home, full of stories about the film, David said he knew a way of letting me see it.

'How?' I asked.

'You'll see.' And he went upstairs.

When I peeped round his bedroom door, he was busily joining several wide strips of paper together with sticky paper.

'What are you doing?'

'Go away. I haven't finished yet.'

'Can't I watch?'

'No. I'll tell you when it's ready.'

But I crept back and saw him drawing and colouring pictures along his roll of paper. And I watched as he cut the front from a cardboard box and a vertical slit on either side. He then carefully decorated around the edges.

'Right, you can see it now,' he said.

I settled down in the playroom as David enthusiastically pulled his pictures through the slots in the decorated box, narrating the action of *Henry V* scene by scene. And Devizes had a cinema.

Grandma had no idea she was a VIP, visiting the gardens at the side of The Meadow, when she judged our family gardening competition, but *we* knew she was judging the Devizes Annual Garden Show.

'She's coming,' we said, and watched her, with notebook and pencil in hand, walking slowly along the edge of our small neat flower beds, making her judgment.

Just before the competition, I poked away at the stony soil with a trowel to remove any last weeds. And occasionally I cycled with the boys to Peckham Market, where we pushed through the crowds to buy small, brightly coloured plants.

'We can't go to Peckham, it's raining,' said David, one Saturday, as he carried a cardboard box into the playroom. We had intended wandering around the market and I had saved sixpence for a new plant. Instead, I followed David into the playroom to see what was in the box.

An elaborate network of roads and hills had been created on the playroom table, and there was a bridge link to the adjacent card table. David and Nigel were taking Dinky cars from the box and setting them in place on the layout. I looked longingly at them all, wishing I could have my own Dinky car, but girls weren't expected to be interested in such things.

'Can I play?' I asked, tentatively.

'It's Devizes,' said Nigel. 'Look, we've got all the roads marked out like the real thing.' So we played Devizes in miniature while the rain beat down outside.

The next Saturday, when I cycled to Herne Hill to do some shopping for Mother, I pressed my nose against the newsagents' window, staring at an unbelievable sight. After years without any metal toys, I saw Buicks, Daimlers, Wolseleys, Rileys, Morgans and Fords — a whole collection of colourful Dinky cars. Slowly I scanned the line wishing I could afford one, but I knew they would be far too expensive.

As I looked at each one in turn, a small green van caught my attention. It was ninepence; the cheapest one there. I've got sixpence, I remembered, and with sudden determination I decided to save up. Twice I cycled to Herne Hill and looked in the shop window, to make sure the small green van was there. But I still only had sixpence, so reluctantly I continued using the boys' cars. Saving was difficult when we often had no pocket money, for times were hard for our parents.

On a hot sunny day soon afterwards, we visited Grandma in her garden, and when it was time to leave Grandma said a surprising thing, 'Buy yourselves an ice cream, dears.'

I watched her give something to David, then to Nigel, and soon my fingers were curling round a small coin.

'Thank you very much, Grandma!' we chorused, thrilled by her unusual generosity, and we cycled off to the Tuck Shop in Dulwich Village. But as I looked at the threepenny-bit pressed into my hand I made an impulsive decision.

'I'm not going to have one!' I said, and leaving the boys staring after me, I cycled on to Herne Hill. Clutching Grandma's threepence and my saved-up sixpence I hurried into the newsagents'.

'That one in the window, please,' I said pointing to the little green van. Proudly I carried it from the shop. I didn't mind that it wasn't even a proper Dinky car — just a hollow shell without a base — and I had missed having an ice cream. For me the sacrifice was worth it.

'*Chemises!*' announced David, one day. 'That's what the allotment can be called in Devizes. It's another town.'

It was such a good word, we just had to use it. 'Muxworthy' was another word that had to be used, so we gave it to Mr and Mrs Deighton's garden, next door, and I was reminded once more of my form mistress in Swansea. Every summer the Butterfields and Nottinghams went to Muxworthy, when Nigel and I were invited in to pick soft, over-ripe gooseberries.

'It's a fruit picking excursion,' I said, popping a squashy gooseberry into my mouth.

But Nigel had other things to think about. 'George's got some cigarettes,' he said, conspiratorially. 'We're going to the field later on to smoke them.'

'Can I come?' I asked hopefully, and as soon as we had finished fruit-picking, I tagged on behind.

We sat in a row with our backs against the spiky hedge of the bombed house. First came George, then David, Rosemary, Ann, Nigel and lastly me. I listened to the coughs and comments as the cigarette passed slowly along the line. Dare I try I wondered, until Nigel handed me the soggy butt. Gingerly I took a puff, then another, choking and spluttering, yet trying to look grown-up. But I much preferred putting two empty extended fingers to my lips, and blowing out an imaginary haze, as we did in Devizes.

Spreading our horizons into the Polytechnic field, we created more 'towns' gleaned from Father's AA map — Andover, Hungerford, Marlborough and Market Cross — with vague boundaries and a network of imaginary roads. David's newly-invented *Progress Magazine* was based at 2 Streatley Mansions, Market Cross, although no such magazine existed, only the headed notepaper of its imaginary publisher.

If Kenneth Butterfield, Michael Ackland, the Fangsters or the Nottinghams went 'logging', the woods and disused tennis courts extended Devizes still further. Occasionally the whole family went logging and we carried back wood on a Y-shaped branch, or on two longer branches used like a stretcher. And whenever we played in the woods, we looked out for more dead branches to drag home to be sawn or chopped ready for winter fires.

When David, Nigel and I left the woods one day, we found our way round the side of the neglected wooden club house by the tennis courts. Ducking under dense leaves we came out into a cricket field.

'What's over there?' said Nigel, indicating a mass of trees and a rough boundary hedge, running along the side of the field. 'Let's have a look.'

We crossed a corner of longer grass and squeezed through a convenient gap in the ragged hedge. Ahead of us, where the canopy of branches parted, I saw a streak of sunlight and a faint sparkle reflecting back from a mass of watery weeds.

'What's that?'

We moved closer in.

'A *river!*' said Nigel.

And there it was; a whole new world. Untamed trees towered above the weed-clogged backwater, and an untidy mass of bushes spilled out on either bank. But for us it held the promise of adventure.

'There's a bridge up there,' said David. And we pushed through thick undergrowth with branches slapping back at us, as they tried to bar our way.

We reached the bridge and hesitantly I followed the boys on to the partly-rotting planks. I gripped a loose chain draped along one side and saw it dipping into the murky water. Its rusty links left a brown stain on my hands as I moved along the dilapidated bridge.

'We could float a raft here,' David said, poking a stick down below the weeds. 'Let's get some wood.'

Soon we were collecting short planks of wood from our usual source, the bombed house, and carrying them back to the river. David bound them together with lengths of knotted string and we lowered our tiny raft into the stagnant water. Cautiously he tested his weight, first one foot, then the other.

'It's still floating. Hand me that bit of plank.' And kneeling on the uneven boards, David manoeuvred his way through the weeds with a smaller piece of wood.

'It's my go next,' said Nigel, as he and I stood on the bank watching the slow progress.

In reach of the bridge David grabbed at a length of dangling chain, but the rusting links came away in his hand, the raft slewed sideways, and he toppled in. From the river rose the rank stench of ancient mud. Then David emerged, draped in weeds, coughing and spluttering. But Nigel and I just laughed and laughed, for each time David reached for the drooping chain he plunged back in, but he went down laughing.

'It's a backwater to the River Effra,' said George, when he later came to see our raft, and we asked him about the secret river. 'It disappears underground a bit further on.'

'What happens to it?' we asked.

'It goes into the Thames at Vauxhall Bridge.'

From then on the River Effra became an extension of Devizes. When I found a black-painted toy gun near the tennis courts, Nigel made one for himself from a piece of wood. Then, as 'bank robbers', we chased across the field to our hiding place by the River.

We had watched the V1 bomb site in Burbage Road being cleared of broken bricks, jagged tiles, glass and splintered wood

— the only remnants of a home. And we had watched a new house being built on the site. Soon the Barratt family moved in, and Peter, a year younger than me, longed to be part of Devizes.

'I think he ought to join,' I said, when Nigel and I were discussing the proposition in the playroom. 'We need more people.'

'He'll be like Rosemary and Ann,' said Nigel, dismissively. 'He won't understand what it's all about.'

But soon we found that small, sandy-haired Peter was a keen stamp collector, and as we had recently started our own stamp club in Devizes, he was eventually allowed to join.

'I'm going to have a sale of swaps,' Peter announced, full of enthusiasm. 'It's at my house. Tomorrow.'

So the next day, Nigel and I went along and pored over the stamp displays, carefully set out on Peter's kitchen table. 'I like these triangular ones,' I said.

'Swaziland. Tonga. Tobago. I haven't got any of these.' Nigel had already lined up his favourites and was looking for more.

Peter was pleased as we selected stamps and he pocketed the Devizes money. Equally delighted, we picked up our stamps ready to leave. But just as we reached the door we spun round, whipping out our guns, and demanded back the money.

'That's not fair!' protested Peter, forgetting to say 'unwodge'.

'Yes it is. Guns are *real* in Devizes.'

Poor Peter was out-numbered and meekly handed over our hand-written notes.

But the next day our mother challenged us. 'You can't keep the stamps,' she said. 'That would be stealing.'

'We bought them,' said Nigel, indignantly.

'And who made the money and then demanded it back?'

Grudgingly we returned Peter's stamps. But we wouldn't let him stay in Devizes after that, and for a while Peter kept his distance.

The sun shone hotly. The clear blue sky held no trace of cloud. It was August. 'I'm going to take the Dinky cars to the tennis courts,' Nigel said. 'You coming?'

He carried the box of cars, with my little green van and some tiny aeroplanes, across the parched field to the tennis courts, where we started manoeuvring them through the weeds and dry hummocky moss. Only one court was disused now, for the tennis club was being re-furbished.

'What's that?' I asked, watching Nigel pulling at a partly-covered strip of greyish metal, displacing weeds as the strip appeared. 'Look, here's some more.' I followed the line across the weed-covered court.

'There's lots of it,' said Nigel.

Rolling up the narrow strips left excellent runways and roads for our tiny aeroplanes and cars, so we played happily for the rest of the morning. When it was time to go home we took the rolled-up strips with us to show David.

'That's lead,' he said. 'We can make coins for Devizes out of it. Get some milk-tops.' He set about melting down the lead strips in an old saucepan on the gas stove. I watched as he carefully poured a small amount of molten metal into each silver-foil milk top, then left them to solidify.

The next time Nigel and I ran across the field to the tennis courts, we saw the stocky figure of our 'elderly' friend Mr Waring, the secretary of the once-thriving club.

We had met Mr Waring on our frequent visits to the woods, and he often gave us twopenny bars of Fry's peppermint cream. He was particularly solicitous towards me, putting his arm around me and cuddling me whenever he could, although I always tried to wriggle away. Once he gave me a lupin plant for my garden, which I tended with care, hoping to win the gardening competition. But today our normally cheerful Mr Waring seemed concerned.

'Have you seen any strangers hanging around?' he asked, with a puzzled frown, as he stared at the tennis courts.

'Strangers?' we queried.

'Yes, thieves have stolen the lead marking lines on this court.'

'Thieves?' 'Marking lines?' we said together, glancing furtively at each other.

'No. No, we haven't seen any *strangers*.' And as soon as we could, we hurried home before there were any more awkward questions.

'What shall we do? Do you think he knows it was us?' I said.

'Of course not, but we've got to hide the evidence. We'll have to use my secret compartment.'

Nigel lifted a loose floorboard in his bedroom doorway, reluctantly revealing his hiding place. Then we filled a two-pound jar with the coins. I knew it was one of Mother's prized Pan-Yan pickle jars she used for her own chutney, but it was the largest we could find, and our needs were more urgent, we decided.

'Steady,' said Nigel, as we lowered the green-lidded jar into the narrow space, 'it'll go through the plaster.' With the jar safely hidden away he firmly replaced the floorboard. 'Anyway,' he added, philosophically, 'they can't use a row of lead coins as marking lines.'

Thankfully, we heard no more about the lead and soon we watched the tennis courts and club house nearing completion. Sheila Moon and I watched too. Sheila and I had met at school and now we had picnics in the woods, tea at each other's houses and shopping trips with our mothers. So once the tennis club re-opened, we gladly joined the junior section.

After my school tennis lessons in the summer term, I had taught Nigel the rules so we could play in the garden. But now the tennis club had opened Nigel joined as well. Despite his age he was soon upgraded to the seniors, while Sheila and I, talking and giggling, continued to pat the ball over the net in the juniors.

'D'you know,' I said to Sheila, proudly, as we ambled back from the courts. 'I taught Nigel to play tennis *and* to play the piano.'

Although I did initially help Nigel learn the notes and some of the exercises, I was struggling with my own weekly piano pieces. In Swansea I had 'shown promise', but here in Dulwich the teacher had no real interest, so my enthusiasm died. Meanwhile Nigel tinkled away happily, picking up tunes and composing too, and to our surprise he started 'cello lessons at school.

'Anyway,' I said, when I finally gave up my lessons. 'I'm going to write a *full length story* instead.'

And with notebook and pencil, I became Hilary Fangster in Devizes, and went off to the seat under the yellow forsythia hedge in Mildew Crescent, to immerse myself in another make-believe world.

10. The Black Rovers: 1946-1947

'I want to have a talk,' said Stuart, just after my twelfth birthday.
It was the beginning of October and I was looking out of the playroom window, watching yellow tinted leaves spiralling from the wispy ash tree and filling the bird bath. I turned round as Stuart came towards me. 'What about?' I said, in surprise.

Stuart was staying in our boxroom while his parents went through the painful process of divorce. So I was used to him always being there, involving himself with Devizes and joining in our many activities. 'You've got to sit down,' he said, guiding me into the old, winged armchair by the garden door. 'I want to ask you something.'

Whatever does he want, I wondered, sitting down dutifully. And he squashed up beside me, slipping his arm around my shoulder.

'Will you be my — girlfriend?' he said, in a hesitant voice.

I hadn't expected that, and giggled nervously. I didn't know what to say. I had always thought Stuart and I would probably marry one day, but that would be a long way off. So to agree to be his girlfriend now seemed far too permanent — although I was pleased he had asked me. Somehow I felt it would be wrong to say 'yes'. After all, supposing I met someone else?

We talked it over, sitting there in the old armchair, with his arm around my shoulder. I didn't want to hurt his feelings by hesitating, but I tried not to say a binding 'yes'. In the end we decided on an 'arrangement' and agreed to walk down Burbage Road together to get our buses for school. But each morning, as we approached Herne Hill railway bridge, Stuart walked on ahead to join his friends going to St Joseph's on Beulah Hill, while I joined mine for St Martin's. Boys thought it was sissy to be seen with girls, although I wouldn't have minded.

Stuart must have told Nigel about our arrangement, for Nigel decided that to make it official Stuart and I should kiss each other *properly*. So while Stuart and I stood face to face and kissed our pursed-lipped kiss, Nigel — making sure we kept going — slowly counted to twenty.

It was not long after this, one Wednesday lunch time, that my class was sent home from school with an important note. I knew what it was about, we had discussed it on the lower netball court. But it put me in a dilemma, because the note asked our mothers to explain the facts of life to us.

'If I tell her I know,' I said to Sheila, as the bus took us back to Herne Hill, 'she'll ask me how I found out. Then she'll say Nigel shouldn't have told me.'

We couldn't find a solution, so I left Sheila to walk home, while I dawdled along Half Moon Lane and up Burbage Road. Finding Mother in the hall, I stood by awkwardly while she read the note.

'We'll have a little chat later,' she said. 'But first I've got something for you.' And she started up the stairs.

I waited apprehensively until she came down again and handed me a slim green book. 'Read this through, then see if you have any questions.'

Escaping to my room with *How Life is Handed On,* I read about the bodily functions of birds, rabbits and other animals, still worrying how to tell her I already knew. But the moment had gone, and when we sat down together in front of the playroom fire, Mother casually said it was the same for people. We were both embarrassed by the whole affair and glad when our little chat was over. Normally 'sex' was *never* mentioned.

'Look! there's the *Golden Arrow!*' David and I were staring across to the far side of the Polytechnic field, watching a shiny green engine hauling its chocolate and cream carriages along the railway embankment.

'The French version's called the *Flèche d'or* and those are Pullman carriages,' explained David, who was fascinated by trains.

'What are Pullman carriages?'

'They're specially equipped with arm rests and tables, and you get meals served while the train's going along.'

This was unimagined luxury when I thought back to our long dreary journey from Swansea. David knew all the train times, so when we were home from school, we dashed upstairs to our parents' bedroom to see this exclusive train, with its golden arrow emblazoned across the front of the engine.

The 'boat train to Paris', as it was called, had re-started early in 1946, but although David spared time to catch a glimpse of it steaming past, by now he was working hard for his school certificate exams. He was also honorary Junior Editor of *The Villager*, the St Barnabas church and community magazine which Father had started. So David wrote what he called a 'feature article' about the *Golden Arrow*.

Nigel and I had our own areas for delivering the magazines, and every month I puffed up College Road to Dulwich Common, with my bundle of Villagers securely tied to the back of my bike. Delivering was voluntary, but that Christmas as I slipped a magazine through the last of my letter boxes, the door opened and a smiling, elderly lady handed me a shilling.

'Happy Christmas, my dear. And thank you for delivering my magazines.'

'Thank you very much!' I said, thrilled by my unexpected wealth. 'And a Happy Christmas to you!' I jumped on my bike and sped home, singing.

Despite frosty mornings, no one could have guessed, as 1946 gave way to 1947, that the country was in for a 'big freeze'. On the night of 23rd January, steadily and silently the blanket of snow fell. By morning, with delight, we found our world had been transformed.

Snow fell on snow, while a raw east wind whipped up huge drifts. At night the temperature dropped still further, leaving the thick covering glazed with frost; then more snow fell on top. By the weekend, the temperature had dropped so low that beautiful frost patterns, covering the bedroom windows, lasted all day and thickened by night. Icy winds had blown through the war-damaged ceilings for the past two winters, sending down showers of dust from the crumbling plaster. But now the thick snow-covering acted like a tea-cosy, keeping out the persistent wind.

On the roads the snow impacted, as vehicles that managed to get through flattened each new covering over the glassy surface below. Even in London, minor roads became impassable. During February the snow continued day after day, with virtually no sunshine. And Big Ben refused to function.

It was a time of sledging and snowmen; snowballs and snow fights. It didn't affect us when we heard that the roads were blocked, cars were covered, and railway lines had to be dug clear. We heard about isolated villages and remote farms being cut-off, and of the RAF dropping supplies to them by parachute, but this all added to the excitement.

As the harsh weather continued, the situation grew worse. Food and supplies were held up, people had difficulty getting to work, and many factories and offices closed. Coal couldn't be moved, so it piled up at the collieries creating an acute shortage. As a result, gas and electricity had to be restricted, and street lighting, illuminated advertisements and shop window lights were banned.

We had electricity cuts every day and candles suddenly became scarce. The BBC's new Third Programme and the recently restarted television channel — for the few who could receive it — were suspended. Newspapers were reduced in size. It was like wartime all over again.

But the heavy snow was an asset for Nigel, Stuart and me. Each evening we went to the kitchen and made thick slices of toast spread with dripping and chutney, then we put on warmed coats, boots, gloves and balaclava helmets. Standing in a circle in the kitchen, the three of us shouted, 'Ick, ack, ock'; our usual way of deciding who would go first on our home-made sledge.

On the word 'Ock' we threw out a hand, showing either spread fingers to indicate 'paper', two open fingers for 'scissors', or a clenched fist for a 'stone'. The winner of this elaborate procedure emerged by a process of elimination.

Sledging with Stuart

'Right, Margaret's turn first,' said Nigel, when my 'paper' had successfully covered their 'stones'.

We went out into the dark, icy evening and dragged our sledge to the gate. I climbed on, sitting with my knees up under my chin, and Stuart tied a scarf round my eyes as a blindfold. The sledge jerked forward through the gateway, and eating our toast and dripping, we moved off, roaming the slippery, snow-covered streets.

I thought I knew exactly where we were going, imagining the roads as I glided along, but being pulled in complete darkness with total trust, gave me an eerie feeling. With ingenious twists and turns, doubling back, sliding over hidden kerbs and even circling round in the road, I became completely lost.

'Where are you now?' I heard Nigel say, and it was always a surprise when I lifted the blindfold to reveal where we were. Nigel and Stuart then recounted each twist in the journey, before one of them gained the return ride.

The 'big freeze' lasted over seven weeks, and during that school term I was absent thirty-three times — either through illness or because I was unable to get there due to the weather. With hills treacherous to walk on, lack of transport and no such thing as gritting and salting we couldn't go far.

Before the snow ended, it gave us a final onslaught in March, and was the worst fall of the winter, breaking many meteorological records. We heard that depths exceeded twelve inches, with drifts up to 30feet in places. But we children loved it.

When the thaw started — accelerated by heavy rain — floods

The thaw started

were the next hazard. We splashed in our boots through the slushy water as it spurted from the overloaded drains and gurgled along the kerbsides. Having been frozen hard for so long, the ground took a long time to thaw, so flood water ran off to further swell the already swollen rivers. The Lord Mayor of London opened a Flood Relief Fund, and St Martin's was among the many contributors, by donating £20 from our 'charities fund'.

'What do you mean, we can't go straight into the seniors now?' As usual several of us were on the lower netball court, discussing important news.
'We've got to take the 11-plus,' someone said.
'What's that?'
'An exam. We've all got to take it.'
'What sort of exam?'
'When?'
'Anyone who doesn't pass can't go into the seniors.'
It sounded ominous to me, but when I told my parents, I realised they already knew. They told me how it was all part of a big educational reorganisation that was taking place, now the earlier 1944 Education Act was being implemented. And St Martin's was to become a Direct Grant School. But they also said, as tactfully as they could, that I just might not be able to continue through the school, because a group of us in the lower third, who were already twelve, were too old to take the new exam.

The possibility of not being able to continue at St Martin's, now I was happily part of it, was unimaginable. Where would I go? Who else would have to leave?

'Don't worry about it,' Mother said, trying to reassure me. 'We don't know yet what will happen. It's all in the air.'

As winter reluctantly slipped into spring, I was able to push the idea further to the back of my mind, when Nigel and I decided to form the *Black Rovers*. With papers strewn across the playroom table, we started work on another magazine, which was to be part of it. This didn't mean the end of Devizes, for by now Devizes had become an institution incapable of extinction. It was there all the time, simmering in our day-to-day lives, even though other interests, and now the Black Rovers, had begun to creep in.

'We'll call our magazine *The Rover*,' said Nigel. 'I'll be the editor and the treasurer and you're the business manager.'

'And the secretary,' I interrupted.

'We can give reports about the Black Rovers and all our activities.'

'And we can do sports and training,' I added.

'I'm Captain and Chief Medical Officer,' Nigel continued, 'and you can be a corporal and the Gym Mistress.'

'Who's going to be the Vice Captain?'

'All right, you can be Vice Captain as well. Stuart can be a lance corporal and the Messenger. And we can use Grandpa's uniforms.'

We had discovered a whole trunkful of Grandpa's red and dark blue service uniforms and other items of khaki army equipment, and with David's help had brought it down from the loft.

'Come on, let's sort them out now,' I said, impatiently. So we raced upstairs and dragged the trunk on to the landing. There had originally been swords and guns too, but we knew our parents had handed these in to West Dulwich Police Station during the war.

'Look, there're some bandoliers. We can have one each.' Delving into the trunk, Nigel pulled them out and hung one diagonally across his chest, while I retrieved a khaki beret and forage cap.

'I'll have the beret and Stuart can have this one,' I said.

Nigel, in his brown jersey and large dark-green corduroy trousers — handed down from a distant relative — was already wearing an officer's peaked cap, while he pulled more intriguing things from the musty-smelling trunk. I liked the khaki webbing belts, with various pouches and attachments to clip on, and later I would sew loops of elastic to my corporal's stripes so I could slip them over my arm.

'Put these on,' Nigel said, handing me two long strips of khaki material.

'What are they?'

'Puttees, of course. They go on your legs like this.' And he bound them tightly round his dark-green trouser legs, in first world war fashion.

I took the puttees and started binding them up my bare legs, from ankle sock to knee. 'This is far better than David's JTC at school!'

David had joined the Junior Training Corps at Alleyn's and every Friday I saw him going off to school in his khaki battledress, with blankoed belt and shiny boots. Nigel would join when he was fourteen, but until then he was content to wear our unique uniform for the Black Rovers, and out in the garden we practised marching, training and rifle drill with long sticks.

'Qui-ick MARCH. Left, right, left, right. Ri-ight WHEEL.' ordered Nigel, as Stuart and I marched round the garden. 'Aa-ten-SHUN. Stand easy.' And sometimes, dressed in full uniform Nigel, Stuart and I marched to Dulwich Park.

Getting money for the Black Rovers was going to be difficult we realised, but we hoped our advertisements displayed on the back page of each magazine would bring in a little.

'We'll charge a shilling for a whole page,' said Nigel, optimistically. 'Sixpence for half a page. A quarter page can be threepence and an eighth page a penny-halfpenny. I've written an eighth page already. Look.'

I read the advertisement Nigel had just finished crayoning: *Good Art = Good Style. Let an experienced Artist draw for you. For particulars apply to the Editor.*

'I'm going to do one for Margaret Green's Needlework Shop,' I said, and went off to my bedroom to think it out. Rashly I started with a quarter page and wrote: *If you have any needlework you would like done please send it to me. Reasonable charges. Good service.* But I soon changed it to an eighth page: *Margaret Green's Needle-*

The Rover.

No.1. Vol.1.   April 10ᵗʰ 1947

Contents.

Forward _____ 1.
Black Rovers News _____ 3.
Puzzle Page _____ 5.
Stranded at the sea side (serial)_____ 6.
Readers Letters _____ 7.

Editor's Letter.

Dear Readers

As you know This is THE FIRST NUMBER of the "Rover". I hope you enjoy it, and do all the puzzles and win a prize. I will be glad of any criticism or any suggestions. Once more I hope you will enjoy this magazine and be a regular subscriber.

The Editor.

2

work. Send any jobs to me.

When cousin Gill from Wallington came to stay with us for half-term, she became a private in the Black Rovers, and the Dramatics Organiser. And we decided that, now there were more of us, we could copy each issue of the magazine several times to give it a wider circulation. We made each one from two double pages secretly pulled from school exercise books, and thought 2d a fair price to charge. Remembering David's serial story in our earlier DVS magazine, I started writing a serial called *Stranded at the Seaside* and drew a picture of two boys waiting forlornly on a railway platform.

'I haven't got time to draw my picture in all the magazines,' I told Nigel. 'It's Sheila's birthday outing. Will you copy it for me?'

'Gill can do it. I'm too busy,' said Nigel, and he carried on writing. Looking over his shoulder, I read: *Handy Hints — Always remember to put cold potatoes away minus a spoon because the spoon will go green.* I didn't stop to read any more.

Sheila Moon's birthday outing to the theatre was a rare occasion for dressing up, so I didn't mind missing Black Rovers' activities. Giggling with excitement, Barbara, Anne, Penny, Annette and I squeezed, sardine-fashion, into the back of Mr Moon's big black Austin. And with Sheila perched on her mother's lap in front, we travelled up to the West End.

The thrill and anticipation were overwhelming, as still giggling and chattering we crowded into the theatre. The lights dimmed, the orchestra struck up and we settled down to enjoy *Oklahoma* — bright, colourful and almost intoxicating after the drabness we had become so used to. We sang the songs and talked about our visit for days afterwards.

At home, while I sang *Oklahoma*, David boomed *The Gondoliers*, because David was in the chorus and Nigel in the orchestra of their school's annual Gilbert and Sullivan performance. Songs were thumped on the piano, hummed whistled and sung. But *Oklahoma* and *The Gondoliers* were only temporary distractions, for lurking at the back of my mind was the prospect of leaving St Martin's. I tried not to think about it, and back in the playroom I temporarily lost myself in copying out my serial story in *The Rover*.

Nigel sat at the other end of the table engrossed in writing, too. 'I'm putting in Telegrams and six lines to make a picture for the Puzzle Page,' he said.

'Telegrams' and 'Six Lines' were two of the many 'paper games' the whole family often played in the evenings. And from time to time Mother pinned up a railway travel poster, as a subject for each of us to write a story. We gave the poster to Grandma and the aunts for their contributions, and afterwards passed round the amazing results for everyone to read. Tired of writing my story in the magazine, I was looking across to the travel poster — still pinned to the wall where the war map used to be — when Mother came bursting into the playroom with the afternoon post.

'Margar, good news,' she said. 'The governors are providing twelve places for some of the juniors to continue through the senior school.'

'Can I go up then?' I said, in delight.

'It means an exam, but if you work hard there's no reason why you shouldn't pass.'

'What sort of exam?'

'The same sort as the 11-plus,' Mother explained. 'It's specially for you older ones who were disrupted by the war. That's why the governors are providing the places.'

It was better news, and I went happily back to my story. But I still had an exam to take. And supposing I didn't pass?

Stuart, in the meantime, successfully passed one of our Black Rovers' tests, and become a corporal. BLACK ROVERS NEWS, a double-page feature in the magazine, gave details of Stuart's success, together with other important news items.

'How does this sound?' Nigel said, and started reading, 'Last week on Saturday 6th April, members of the Black Rovers held their first sports class of the season. Under the direction of Corporal Margaret Green, they spent a happy hour running, jumping, skipping and playing football. We hope to do this regularly every Saturday, if the weather permits.'

'Yes, that's good,' I agreed, remembering how the boys had insisted on playing football.

We often played football in the Polytechnic field behind the house. Stuart, Nigel and I spaced out two coats on the grass for a goal, and one of us would be goalkeeper with the other two as opposing 'teams'. When Gill stayed with us she played too, and we learnt to tackle and dribble; to head and trap; to score and save goals. Gill and I became almost as fast and almost as skillful as the boys.

Sometimes we saw the irate groundsman, over by the pavilion, shouting at us and waving his arms to make us go away. If we ignored his warning a tractor started heading towards us. Then we picked up the ball, grabbed our coats and ran. If we reached the solitary tree in the field before the groundsman reached us, we knew we could make it to the hole in the fence and the safety of the tennis courts. But the tractor usually turned back once we started running.

After that, we played on the cricket field bordered by Gallery Road, the woods and the River Effra — until the next time we dared return to taunt the groundsman. Having been chased off the Polytechnic field one Saturday, Nigel, Stuart and I set up our coats in the cricket field and re-started the game.

'Look at those three boys over there, watching us,' said Stuart, jerking his head towards Gallery Road.

The boys were leaning on the fence, but as we looked they climbed over and came towards us. 'Can we play?' one of them asked.

So we formed two teams — them and us — to continue the game. I was keeping well up with the others and enjoying the game, when one boy kicked the ball hard towards the fence and all three ran after it. They picked up the ball and were clambering back into Gallery Road before we realised what was happening.

'That's my ball!' shouted Stuart.

'Come on after them!' Nigel started running, so we chased across the field shouting as we ran. But it was no use. The ball had gone. Picking up our coats we walked disconsolately home, discussing what we would do to the three boys if we ever caught them.

Until Mrs Mac bought Stuart a new football, we practised long and high jump, sack and obstacle races, and 100-yard sprints to the tree in the field. This surge of activity, under the direction of Corporal Margaret Green, led towards our Sports Day planned for the summer holidays. At the same time, in a sudden burst of enthusiasm, Nigel organised a weekly nature class to study plants and animal life. 'Birds' was the subject of the first meeting, duly reported in our magazine. The report ended: *Readers are invited to see a good collection of nature books in the editor's bedroom.*

'We still need more money. We can't do anything without money,' complained Nigel one day. 'And no one wants a full-page advert,' he added, gloomily.

'We could have a sale,' I suggested.

We were in the playroom discussing the problem.

'In aid of the Black Rovers Fund! Yes, that should bring some money in.'

So Nigel wrote a notice in the magazine, adding an eye-catching postscript, thickly written in red crayon. Then we prepared for the big day. Stuart sorted out some books he didn't want. Nigel made note pads and packaged up foreign stamps. I embroidered stencilled flowers on a tray cloth and made bracelets from Mother's discarded 'whale bones' from her corsets.

The following Saturday, Nigel, Stuart and I pushed back the chairs in the playroom and spread our odd assortment of hand-made, unwanted and purloined goods over the table.

'The customers are waiting in the hall,' I said, hearing muted voices.

'Can't open 'til three. It says so in the magazine,' Nigel insisted.

'Who's taking the money?' asked Stuart.

'We all are. Just sell what you can.'

As soon as the grandfather clock chimed three, we declared our sale open. Grandma came in first, followed by the aunts, Mrs Mac, David and our parents. We stood by watching them viewing the ill-assorted collection. Then came Mother's friend, Mrs Holgate, with her son Gerald, who was in Nigel's year at school.

'A *book-mark*, Margaret dear,' said Auntie Madge. 'That's *just* what I need.'

'Who's been raiding the larder?' laughed Mother, buying back a packet of jelly.

Mrs Holgate bought a 'whale-bone' bracelet.

We noticed other items being discreetly placed on the table by the buyers, and by the end of the afternoon we eagerly counted our takings. 'Six shillings and threepence!' we proudly announced.

Now we were solvent, we felt the Black Rovers had a greater status. We took on more activities and marched in single file to the woods to continue our training. I came upon the woods each spring with renewed delight — the bright freshness of grass and weeds springing up under foot; trees bursting into leaf; birds chattering amongst themselves in a hidden green world.

We stalked and hid, climbed trees and constructed camps under their drooping branches. We made catapults and shaped wood into bows and arrows. And bramble-scratched and muddy, we crawled through the undergrowth to 'spy' on the tennis and cricket clubs.

Crouching in a tight thicket of bushes, Stuart and I heard Nigel's whistle for identification as he returned from a vital reconnaissance. He had taught me the secret whistle, a simple tune on four notes for the call, with an answering tune on three. I gave the answering call, hoping our hiding place wouldn't be discovered by the 'Red Marauders' before Nigel could reach it. David and George had become the Red Marauders, but they quickly decided it was far too childish.

Back at home in the playroom, we tapped out Morse code messages on tiny Morse code keys. And I carefully cut scraps of material into small semaphore flags and tied them to sticks. Then from one end of the garden to the other, we waved our way through many secret messages, until the novelty wore off. Knots and how to use them, and the intricacies of codes and coded messages were equally important.

'All Black Rovers have got to climb out of your bedroom window and down the porch,' Nigel suddenly announced. 'It's an initiative test.'

This development came after we had been playing 'truth, dare or promise' and I hadn't accepted the dare. But now, wearing my school gym shoes, I followed Nigel out through the window. I didn't look down at the front garden, but clung tightly to the frame as I moved a few tiles along.

'Come on,' said Nigel, making his way to the edge of the porch roof. 'You've got to get back through this window.'

Gradually I learnt to ease my way down the sloping tiles, then climb in through the window by the bend in the stairs. I tried not to think about what would happen if I fell.

To give our stamp club greater status we re-launched it through the Black Rovers as the Philatelist Club, under the direction of Captain Nigel Green. Our magazine reported the meetings, and Nigel included a quarter-page advertisement offering four free stamps for $2^1/_2$d postage. He copied the wording from similar adverts he had read in his *Beano* and *Dandy*.

'Can I join the Black Rovers?' Peter Barratt asked one day, when he found us busily writing in the playroom. Being a member of the Black Rovers entitled him to join the Philatelist Club, so he had forgiven us our earlier stamp incident with the 'armed hold-up'. We gladly forgot too, and Peter was allowed to join.

In holidays or half-terms we temporarily shelved Black Rovers' activities, when one or two of us went with Father on his business travels round the country in a small Austin Seven van. We visited seaside resorts and country towns — Bournemouth and Yarmouth, Salisbury and Canterbury, Honiton and Lynton. So when David went off to his school's JTC camp near Thetford, Nigel and I had a chance to go away too.

With Nigel perched in the back, the little van bumped along the unfamiliar roads. I looked out for the AA man on his yellow motorbike and sidecar, and waved back eagerly to his smart salute. At the end of each day Father found somewhere to put up our small tent, in a field or even on the grass verge by the roadside. Then his new primus stove popped and spluttered into action as he boiled up the kettle and we ate a picnic meal. We slept soundly on firm ground, waking to see a sparkling bloom covering the grass. And I breathed in the fresh early morning, with a wonderful *I'm on holiday* feeling.

During term-time Father went on these journeys alone, sending home frequent postcards which I collected in an old shoe box. And when he returned we heard stories of his travels. He sat at the playroom table, drinking his usual large cup of tea, while we listened to his latest exploits.

'I caught the Isle of Wight car ferry, ready for an early start in the morning,' he related. 'But a thick mist came down as we travelled across the Solent. By the time I drove off the ferry on to

Father camped on his own

the island I could barely see the road in front of me.'

Sitting in the old winged armchair, I listen to his long-drawn-out story, imagining the little maroon van jolting along the roads.

'I knew I wouldn't be able to find anywhere to stay for the night, so I was glad of the tent.' Father paused to drink his tea, then with great enthusiasm told how he had edged his way along the fog-bound road until he could bump on to the grass. In dense fog he set up his tiny tent and struggled with the primus for a cup of tea and a snack meal, before settling down for the night.

Next morning as he woke, a shaft of sunlight squeezed in through the crack in the tent flaps. The fog had cleared and he could hear the nearby sound of traffic. He climbed out of his makeshift bed, and partly dressed stepped out into the bright morning.

It was only then he realised, to the amazement of passing drivers, that he had pitched his tent on a small traffic island.

As I walked through the hall, I heard my parents talking in the dining room. The door was open and I could hear them discussing a letter which had arrived earlier. They were saying how relieved they were that I would be moving up to the senior school next term. I was delighted I had passed the exam, too, but I wondered who would be moving up with me and who would have to leave.

I was about to go upstairs when they said something about a holiday house on the edge of Whitstable beach. *Beach*, that sounded good, so I stopped briefly to hear more. But they seemed to think it would be too expensive for us all to travel by train. Even so, as I climbed the stairs I still hoped they would say we could go.

Eventually they found a solution. Mother would travel by train, they said, with Nigel to help with the luggage, while Father, David and I would cycle. I didn't mind, as I enjoyed cycling, and even though none of the bikes had gears, the 60-mile journey to Whitstable seemed a reasonable undertaking.

152

11. Beyond the War: 1947-1948

We set off early. Father planned all journeys meticulously and all journeys started early. He studied the map beforehand and wrote out a detailed itinerary, showing the anticipated time of arrival at places along the route. He added noteworthy landmarks which he pointed out, so that as we passed each one our journey was seen to be getting shorter.

Even earlier that morning he had made his 'special' sandwiches. We called them 'special' because they were so impeccably made, with cut-off crusts which we had already eaten. The packets of sandwiches had been stowed, together with maps, drinks, cycle repairs and first aid kit, in a box strapped to the carrier on the back of Father's bike. We joked about his elaborate preparations, but we joked more about his 'holiday clothes', particularly his black well-polished, lace-up shoes, knee-length fawn socks with a wide turn-over and long khaki ex-RAF shorts.

'Only boys in junior schools wear *shorts*,' we said. But Father only laughed.

I was excited about going on holiday, although secretly my excitement was tinged with apprehension in case I couldn't make the journey. Even so, I was proud the others thought I could as we cycled along the empty roads through Forrest Hill, Catford and Eltham to join the A2 to Kent.

'Once we join the ribbon road, there'll be a cycle track along the side for some of the way.' Father called all major roads ribbon roads. 'Then it's downhill all the way to the sea!'

I knew he was making light of the journey and there would be many hills to struggle up, but there was little traffic and only the occasional lorry rattled past. So we cycled on, mile after mile, with the road stretching ahead as far as we could see.

'Just over the brow of the next hill we'll stop for a drink,' came Father's welcome voice, and with head down I kept on cycling.

As we neared Sittingbourne and Faversham our stops became more frequent, and the detailed timetable was long forgotten.

Once, when we topped a hill, we came across a welcome transport café and stopped for a much needed cup of tea and a bun. Then starting to stiffen, and sore of seat, we cycled on for Whitstable.

'Keep going. It's not much further,' encouraged David, and he took turns to give me a helping push. At one point they both pushed me, as we straddled the empty road.

Very overdue, according to the itinerary, we reached West Beach, and Mother and Nigel hurried out to meet us. 'Now, Margar, a nice rest and a cup of tea for you,' said Mother, hustling us all indoors.

But I hadn't cycled all that way just to have a rest, and soon I was watching the sea crashing on the steeply shelved beach, almost up to the back of the house. A few days after we arrived, cousin Gill came down by train to join us, and when the tide was high the four of us jumped and splashed in the towering waves. When the tide was low, Gill and the boys swam.

Before the holiday I had taught Nigel the rudiments of swimming, because I had been having swimming lessons during the summer term. In the school gym we were shown arm and leg movements with the breathing that co-ordinated them.

'Lie over a chair at home and practise the movements,' Miss Imlach, the PE mistress, had said. 'And submerge your face in a basin of cold water — then open your eyes.'

All this I had relayed to Nigel and he practised under my supervision. But I also had weekly trips to the nearest public

Low tide at West Beach

swimming baths. These trips from school, we were told, were a temporary measure until we had enough money to have our own school pool built. To raise the money we held fêtes, sales and all kinds of entertainments, with the enthusiastic encouragement: 'It's for the *swimming bath fund'*. But until it could be built we travelled to East Dulwich for swimming lessons.

I hated those three-mile trips in a green London County Council coach, anticipating what was to come. I hated the echoey white tiled baths, gingerly sliding in and finding space amongst the splashing bodies. But most of all I hated the strong smell of chlorine that made me choke and splutter when water went in my mouth or stung my eyes. So I made all kinds of excuses for not swimming.

Finally, knowing it was an unbreakable rule that we must wear an 'extra garment' after swimming — to prevent catching cold — I said I had forgotten mine. Quietly aware of all our tricks, Miss Imlach had lent me her voluminous stripy cardigan. The humiliation of sidling round the school for two hours, in that stripy cardigan, quickly ended my excuses. But I didn't learn to swim on those school outings, even though Nigel remembered my tuition and now swam with David and Gill.

Some days, sharing the two bicycles, the four of us walked and cycled as we explored the neighbouring roads. David wanted to draw the old windmill for an article he was writing for *The Junior Villager*, so I said I would draw it too and we cycled up the hill with our pencils and sketch pads. After supper, if we didn't wander

The old windmill

round Whitstable, we read books, watched the sea or played our favourite 'paper games' with our parents.

'How about Rhyming Couplets?' suggested David one evening, when we were deciding what to do.

'What's that?' asked Gill.

'It's easy. You play it on long strips of paper, like consequences or heads, bodies and legs.'

'I've got some paper we can use.' Gill was already tearing pages from a notebook. 'What do we have to do?'

'The clock struck two at half past four, and Nelly Atkins slammed the door! That's the sort of thing you've got to write. Then turn the top line over and pass the strip to the next person to write two more lines. We'll try it.'

I remembered David's two lines, because we had played the game before, but my meter was often questionable. As we played, I heard the tinkling notes of a piano being practised in the adjoining house and my mind wandered off the rhyme I was trying to create.

'What's that music called?' I asked Mother, who was busily writing her own verse.

'Clair de Lune,' she said. 'It's by Debussy.'

As soon as the game was over, I slipped outside to our ground floor verandah to hear the music more clearly. Standing there in the warm air, I listened as the haunting tune took shape. And filled with a surge of emotion I wished I hadn't given up my own piano lessons. But the next day the music was forgotten when Gill and I set off to do some window-shopping in the town. As we stopped by one shop we noticed a boy of about Gill's age, idly dawdling along the road — noticing us, too.

'If we walk along slowly,' said Gill, 'we'll meet him. Don't make it look obvious.' And gradually the three of us drew closer, until we found we were looking in the same shop window, so we started to talk.

'Boys', to me, meant Stuart or friends of David and Nigel. I always supposed I would marry Stuart one day, because he was Stuart. David's friends I admired from a distance, old and unattainable, while Nigel's friends were just Nigel's friends — except for good looking, curly-haired Colin.

I thought of Colin and how I had sent him little notes on small scraps of paper, via Nigel. That was when Nigel wrote to Gloria

Gorringe, via me. And I remembered my last birthday party, when Colin had given me a necklace made of seven Bakelite red roses on a narrow gilt chain. But my little notes to Colin had tailed off when I seldom got one back. And Nigel's notes stopped when Gloria left St Martin's.

Now, here I was with Gill talking to an unknown boy! We arranged to meet on other occasions and usually walked arm-in-arm, one of either side of him, along the High Street or up the hill to the windmill.

'We're going to be ever so late if we don't hurry,' I said to Gill one lunch time, as we started back to West Beach after our latest assignation. We were hurrying along the road when we saw David speeding towards us on his bike. He had come to warn us that Father had seen us in the High Street with the boy, and we were in for trouble. Gill seemed unconcerned, but I slunk anxiously back to the house. I had never 'gone out with' a boy before.

'They'll want to know who he is and how we met and all kinds of things,' I said, glumly. Despite my 'arrangement' with Stuart, I knew the very idea of boy and girl friends at my age was almost inconceivable. So to be seen arm-in-arm with a strange boy seemed a mortal crime.

As Gill and I walked into the kitchen I expected Father to say something to us. But he didn't. We sat through lunch and the others chatted as usual, while I thought of an excuse. At one point, when the conversation turned towards the High Street, David deftly changed the subject, and Father didn't pursue it.

After lunch I waited. Now he'll say something, I thought. But there was no reprimand as I had expected, and he only casually mentioned our meetings. So for the rest of our holiday Gill and I continued to meet the boy. And to my innocent twelve-year-old mind I really had a boyfriend. Temporarily I forgot Stuart; after all he was almost part of the family.

As soon as we returned home from Whitstable, David rushed into the garden to check the nine tiny melon plants he had sewn from seed earlier in the year. Nigel and I had laughed about David and his plants, and how he had persuaded Auntie Gladys to stay at the house to water them while we were away.

But David intended writing an article about his latest gardening experiment, and later, forgetting our laughter, we proudly read his article in the threepenny weekly magazine, *Popular Gardening*.

'Daddy and I are going to the George Hotel in Marlow,' announced Mother, towards the end of the summer holidays. I knew they had been planning a short holiday together — the first for many years — and now the arrangements were complete. 'You and Nigel will be sensible and do what David says, won't you? I'm relying on you.'

'Yes, of course we will.' A week on our own; the prospect sounded promising, until Mother added:

'Auntie Flo will be coming to stay. . .'

'Auntie *Flo?* But you said we'd be on our own.'

'She'll be staying each night.'

'Does she *have* to?'

'Yes, she does. But on the Saturday you can come down by train for the day, and we'll meet you at the station.'

On the first evening, when Auntie Flo arrived, I was surprised when she said in her 'correct' voice, 'I shall give sixpence, dears, to the first one who is undressed and downstairs ready to say goodnight.'

David wasn't included, so on our way upstairs to undress Nigel and I agreed that whoever was ready first should wait on the landing for the other one. 'If we go downstairs together,' said Nigel, 'we'll both get sixpence.'

And it worked!

Auntie Flo left early each morning for her office and arrived after supper, so we enjoyed our week of freedom, getting up when we wanted and eating when we liked. Time flashed by and soon we were tidying the house and preparing for our visit to Marlow.

'Let's make a special meal for when they come home,' I suggested.

'We've eaten everything!' said Nigel.

'I'll make something.' David was searching through the gas refrigerator, one of our prized possessions from Grandpa's house.

'What sort of thing?' Nigel persisted.

'You'll see.'

On the final Saturday, David wore his new sports jacket and Nigel wore David's outgrown one, while I dressed in my school uniform for 'best'. We travelled down to Marlow from Paddington and saw our parents waiting at the station to meet us. Then we set off to explore the picturesque town. We wandered along the towpath by the gently flowing Thames, and sat on the bank to eat a picnic lunch, watching the occasional boat gliding by.

'Why has that punt got loops over the top of it?' I asked.

'They're for the awning,' said Father. 'The awning's tied up in the daytime and pulled down at night.'

'At night?'

'Yes, for sleeping.'

Sleeping in that small boat under the awning sounded perfect, and we all started talking about what it would be like to 'camp' on the river. Still talking about the river, we found our way to the house where we used to live before the war, and walked up a rough track by the side. But I didn't remember it, for I was barely a year old when we left Marlow. Father took a photograph of the three of us outside the house, with David's Brownie box camera, before we hurried back to the station for the journey home.

Auntie Flo called in that evening to report, 'They were as good as gold, dears. And there wasn't a *tupe* out of them!' Nigel and I remembered our sixpences, but we went on wondering what a 'tupe' could be.

The next day I carefully set the playroom table for the special meal which David had planned. It smelt delicious as he brought it in from the kitchen, but we were amazed to see the extraordinary puce-coloured concoction he placed on the table in front of us.

'It looks *lovely*, David,' said Mother. 'But what did you put in it?'

'Everything. I minced up all the leftovers from meals we had

We stood outside our old house

during the week. Odd bits of vegetable and meat — and all the beetroot.'

'Beetroot!' we chorused in surprise. Even so, we tucked in heartily, enjoying the unusual meal.

In September I 'moved up' to the senior school, with many unfamiliar subjects. We used books blackened by fire and crinkled with water from the bomb damage three years earlier, and we went from room to room for lessons now, lining up quietly outside the door until the black-gowned mistress called us in.

At the start of the term, we crowded into the gym to make sure our uniforms were correct in every detail. The old square-necked gym slip had been replaced by a more modern style, with shirt and tie. But when I heard about the uniform inspection, I had begged Mother to let me wear anything other than my thick lisle stockings, that kept slipping down and wrinkling round my ankles.

'Everyone wears ankle socks,' I insisted.

'But your legs will get so cold.'

'*Please.*'

Reluctantly, although I knew she wasn't happy about it, Mother said I needn't wear the stockings. 'But you must wear long socks to keep your legs warm,' she added.

These were better, and many girls did wear them in the winter, but they were not what I wanted to wear. After the inspection, although I started off from home in my knee-length fawn socks, by the time I reached school I had folded them down to look like ankle socks. Soon after, I cut the centre section from the socks, carefully sewed the other two pieces together and turned the top over the neat row of stitches. I was happy then!

Shoes were another problem because of the lack of clothing coupons, which were still needed. But Nigel and I found a temporary solution. We made cardboard insoles when holes appeared in the soles. When it rained the cardboard slowly disintegrated, and we felt our socks soaking up the wet on the ball of each foot. And when the cardboard wore away we made new insoles, until we were able to go to Oakley's in Herne Hill to buy a new pair of shoes. But however battered the shoes, they always had to be well polished, including the instep.

Whispers of excitement rippled through the school hall one morning, when Miss Gordon Ewen announced that twelve German girls and their teacher, Frau Geldmacher, would be coming to stay for three weeks. 'This is not just a holiday,' continued Miss Gordon Ewen, in her calm, firm voice. 'We will be shaping the future of the world.'

This sounded an ambitious aim, but after the war it had been a priority to create friendly relations with the German people, especially the children, so St Martin's had 'adopted' a school near Lubeck. We exchanged news and sent parcels of books and clothes to the girls. And now some of them were coming to stay.

Host families were needed, but as none of my family spoke German, we weren't selected. Even so, I was delighted when I was allowed to join the 'German Group' as a back-up in case one of the other families should drop out. I enjoyed missing afternoon school, going off in the coach and getting to know the German girls, without the full responsibility of entertaining one of them.

We saw Windsor Castle, Westminster Abbey, St Paul's Cathedral, the Tower of London and the British Museum. We also saw stark bomb sites, where rosebay willow herb and patches of thistles flowered incongruously. As I looked at the derelict ruins, I wondered what Lydia, Ursel, Renate, Hilderuth and Ingrid thought, for they had their own bomb damage and deprivation at home.

To round off their visit we were told there would be a special service at St Martin-in-the-Fields church. 'Outings' such as this, and Founders' Day and carol services, were supposed to be serious occasions, but to us they had become highlight of the year.

We travelled by coach and lined up on a nearby bomb-site to be checked, before our long brown crocodile wound into the church. It was far more fun than lessons, and by the end of the service the church rang out with 500 voices chorusing the school song: 'St Martin through the fields did pass, when snow lay white one candlemas. . .'

Back at home in the playroom, I joined in with another kind of music. Nigel used his 'cello as a double-base, David strummed on the piano while trying to play the comb and paper, and Stuart and I experimented with an assortment of homemade percussion instruments; banging, shaking and thumping. We all took turns to tap out a rhythm on the xylophone to add to our 'music', and by trial and error found that the folded card table made a vibrant thump when we hit it with the palm of the hand. Thimbled fingers skating over Mother's washboard clattered another striking sound.

'We can use this as well,' I said, banging Grandpa's small dinner gong, which I normally used with gusto to announce meals.

It was not long after one of these 'jam sessions', that David and Nigel decided to start the *Burbage Musical Society*. They discussed the details at length, and David typed out a neat list of 'Benefits on Joining'. They gave me a copy, which I read through:

1. You are regularly informed of good musical programmes on the radio worth hearing.
2. You may join the quartet.
3. You are supplied with musical requisites (music, manuscript paper etc.) for reduced prices.
4. You are allowed to come to concerts given by the society free of charge, and take part in them.
5. You may learn an instrument for reduced fees.
6. You are given picture-portraits of the famous composers on request.
7. Any question (genuine) to do with music is answered free of charge.
8. You are able to get free tickets for shows.
9. We lend out music books free of charge.

I duly joined their society, although I didn't take advantage of all the ambitious benefits on offer, because now I was in the seniors I was able to join the school's music club, organised by Miss Copland, the music teacher.

'Once round Miss Copland, twice round the gasometer!' we chanted as we ran, shrieking with laughter, round the lower netball court, although we liked and respected our music teacher.

Each morning at school assembly, Miss Copland — large and round with a head which appeared too small for her ample body — played the grand piano while we sat cross-legged on the hall floor. Sometimes she played requests, provided they were suitable. But the soothing sounds of Chopin, Liszt, Schumann or Bach ended with our clattering feet, when we stood up just before Miss Gordon Ewen glided on to the platform for prayers.

During singing lessons, or hymn practice, the piano stopped abruptly if a word like 'tuss' rang out. Unsmiling, Miss Copland stared at the faces clustered in front of her and we stared back.

'*Let* us. *Let* us. LET us.' she would say in an exaggerated voice. And we repeated the words several times to her satisfaction, before we resumed our singing.

I enjoyed singing hymns and sea shanties, the 'Wraggle Taggle Gypsies' and other old songs. I also enjoyed going with Mother to Alleyn's School concerts. But it wasn't just the music or Nigel playing his 'cello that I went to hear — going to the boys' school meant seeing all the boys! Dressed neatly in school uniform and my hair brushed with extra care, I watched their Shakespearean play each autumn term, too.

More interesting was Alleyn's Founders' Day, when wearing the traditional blue cornflower, picked from the front garden, I wandered round the school grounds with my parents. We watched cricket matches or I found my way to the buttery for tea and cakes, but I seldom plucked up courage to speak to any of the boys.

'I've got to have a Bournville cocoa label, a Cadbury's chocolate label and a 3d stamp,' I said to Mother, when I found her in the kitchen one morning, stacking away the shopping.

'Whatever for?'

'I want to join the C-Cubs.'

'C-Cubs?'

'It's short for Cadbury Cubs. I'll buy the stamp, but I need the labels.'

In time I received my C-Cub badge, a membership book and a lavishly coloured, twelve-page magazine. 'I can collect special C-Cub stamps,' I told Mother. 'If I write a story I'll get an author's stamp.'

I sent in a story and for an artist's stamp copied the chocolate advertisement, showing a glass of milk being poured into a bar of chocolate. I didn't buy any more chocolate because of sweet rationing, but I looked forward, eagerly, to the lively magazine arriving.

'It's Dick Barton!' Nigel yelled up to me, when I was tucked away in my bedroom, reading the latest adventure of Colin, Carol and Chris.

I was so engrossed with the magazine, I had nearly forgotten *Dick Barton, Special Agent*. I leapt down the stairs to the dining room, with 'Devil's Gallop', the signature tune, issuing from the radio. And filled with anticipation, I waited to hear how Dick Barton, with Snowy and Jock, extricated themselves from the most hair-raising situations.

The pace, the excitement, the tension mounted, and by the end of the fifteen minute episode they were left in an even more unlikely state. At school we discussed every twist in the plot, and all possible solutions. With Dick Barton we had entered an exciting new world. But the exciting new world only partly alleviated the pang of disappointment I felt, when I heard that Stuart was moving away.

Stuart had often talked about leaving school as soon as he could, and living on a farm in Gloucestershire. Although he always spent his holidays there and I was vaguely prepared, it was a big wrench when he said he was actually going.

'We can write,' we said. But sadly we quickly lost contact as Stuart found a new way of life on the farm.

Stuart's going gradually merged into the past, when first Uncle Keith's fiancée, then cousin Sheila from Dorking, temporarily occupied the spare room. And during the summer term, David's French pen-friend, Maurice Milard, came to stay. With Maurice we all visited the London museums, Madam Tussaud's and several art galleries, catching up with outings we had missed during the war. As we tramped round the streets, I stared up at the tall scaffolding-covered buildings surrounded by busy workmen, clanking cranes, cement mixers and a flurry of noisy activity.

Despite the activity, in some ways it seemed as though little had changed since the end of the war. There were still bomb-sites, piles of rubble and shattered buildings with jagged protruding floors. Clothes, food, petrol, soap and sweets continued to be rationed, and even bread had been added to the list. But we had grown used to it all and didn't let it affect us.

Looking out of my bedroom window to the house over the crossroads one day, I called out to Nigel, 'They're in their front garden now.'

'Right. Come on let's get the apples,' he said, coming out of his room. He thundered down the stairs and I charged down after him. Nigel gathered up a bucket, then we ran to the fruit trees to scrabble around looking for tiny windfalls.

'That'll do. I'll get my racquet,' he said, and raced back to the house. 'Don't let them see you,' he called, as I cautiously carried the bucket of apples round to the front garden.

A few days earlier we had watched a removal van arriving at the house over the crossroads, and we had seen a slim, dark-haired girl, a little older than Nigel, and a boy of about my age move in.

But we still hadn't made contact with them. Now, crouching down behind the front gate, Nigel lobbed the 'ammunition' over the crossroads with an old tennis racquet, while I kept him supplied. As the bombardment of tiny apples showered down on them, Gwendoline and Roger came to see what we were doing.

After this first meeting, Nigel and I put our old Black Rovers' training into practice again, to spy on them undetected. But as we got to know them, we communicated across the road with flashing mirrors reflecting the sun, and with torches at night. Then someone thought of the matchbox note container.

'We'll need yards of string,' said Roger. 'To thread through the matchbox.' So we stretched the string in a loop from stairs window to stairs window over the wide crossroads — a slow, laborious job, but luckily there was little traffic. When, at last, the string was in place we took turns to pull on the loop, until we could retrieve the matchbox and the note inside.

I didn't really like it when Gwendoline, Roger and Nigel practised the piano, violin and 'cello together. Occasionally they persuaded me to stand by the piano to turn the pages of the music for Gwendoline, but more often I went off on my own to continue my 'full length story'.

Sitting on the low wooden seat under the forsythia hedge in 'Mildew Crescent', I scribbled happily in a hard-covered note-book. But I was most indignant when the others finished their

String stretched across the crossroads

music, and peering over my shoulder accused me of copying Enid Blyton. They had seen my chapter headed 'A nice ending to a horrid day!'.

After our journey to Whitstable the previous year, cycling to Henley-on-Thames seemed an easier undertaking. We had talked of camping on the river ever since our visit to Marlow. Mother and I had even had a 'trial run', earlier in the year, with Auntie Madge. So with this success behind us, Father hired two camping punts for two weeks summer holiday. Because of all the bedding, food and cooking gear which we had to take with us, Mother, with Nigel to help, travelled in a hired car. And this time a school friend of David's cycled with Father, David and me.

We set off, early as usual, cycling happily along the almost empty roads. Petrol was still rationed, and most new cars were for export only, so there was little traffic to worry us. Now and then we saw a postman propping his bike against the kerb and going from house to house, and sometimes we caught up with the electric milk float as it frequently stopped and started.

The journey took us out of London, through Clapham, Putney and Hounslow, to join the A4 Bath Road. It was then easy cycling through Colnbrook and on to Slough and Maidenhead. Occasionally the sun peeped from a cloudy sky, but we could see threatening rain clouds gathering.

All went well until we reached Maidenhead Bridge, when without warning I found myself flying through the air over the handlebars. Father, bringing up the rear, almost collided with me as I landed in a heap on the dusty road. While I was being extricated from my damaged bike, the boys hurriedly cycled back to see what had happened. They sat me on the pavement and found I was shaken and dizzy but otherwise unharmed.

'It's the front mudguard,' David said. 'It must have come off and spun round with the wheel.' He made the bicycle temporarily roadworthy, leaving the offending mudguard by the roadside, then we walked the last few yards into Maidenhead High Street.

'We'll find a chemist to check you over,' said Father, as we pushed our bikes along the pavement.

The chemist sat me on a chair and gave me a small glass of clear bitter liquid. 'Drink it down, it's sal volatile,' he said, fussing over me. 'Nothing's broken, so you'll soon feel better.'

As I hadn't landed on my head, I was pronounced fit to cycle on to Henley. Somewhere along the route we were expecting to be overtaken by the hired car with Mother and Nigel, and pushing slowly up the narrow tree-lined hill from Hurley, we heard a distant engine. Soon we were waving down the loaded car, I hopped in the back with Mother, to be driven the last few miles, while Nigel cycled the rest of the journey on my dilapidated bicycle. When we met up again, David said they had left the bike at a cycle shop for repairs, ready for the return trip.

Leaving the other bikes propped against a fence in the boat yard, we piled our luggage into two gently-rocking camping punts and climbed in, unsteadily. We settled ourselves amongst our neatly stowed boxes and packages and pushed off from the bank, heading upstream one behind the other. It was then that the clouds burst.

All we could do was paddle towards the opposite bank as fast as we could. We gained protection from the driving rain under overhanging trees, tied up and struggled with the two awnings. Feeling surprisingly warm and dry, I listened to the drumming on our taut roof, and peered under the awning to watch the surface of the water churned up by pounding raindrops.

'At least we can eat,' Father said, leaning over the back of the seat as he searched through boxes. With difficulty in our cramped quarters, we prepared a simple meal, passing plates between the two punts and trying to keep the food dry.

'It was just like this on our holiday with Auntie Madge, wasn't it, Margar?' And we recounted, once more, the time earlier that year, when Mother, Auntie Madge and I had spent a crazy weekend on the river.

Setting off from the boat yard had caused cheers and hoots of laughter from a cluster of onlookers on the bank. 'That's it, ladies, you're doing fine,' someone had shouted.

'Keep it up!'

Sitting side by side in the bow of the punt Auntie Madge and Mother dipped their paddles into the water. But instead of being propelled forward with each thrust of the paddles, the unwieldy boat veered from side to side behind them. Then Auntie Madge began to giggle.

'Ignore them, Madge, just ignore them.'

'But, Lilian dear, we're going round in circles!'

'We're not pulling *together*.'

'It's the boat, Lilian, it shouldn't be. . .'

'Madge, whatever are you. . .'

'It's back to front.'

'What's back to. . . *Don't* stand up.'

'But, Lilian dear, we should be sitting at the back!'

Swinging first one way and then the other, we zig-zagged to the opposite bank. I scrambled from the boat to tie it up, and we had waited, hoping another punt would go by so we could see how it should be steered. But it was good practice for our family holiday.

'What are you all laughing at in there?' called David from the other punt.

'Have you got any matches?' interrupted Nigel. 'We can't see a thing.'

Father lit our paraffin lamp and hung it from the central strut that carried the awning, then passed the matches through to the boys in the other boat. Later, in the dim light, we made up beds along the body of each boat. It felt hard at first, as I lay down on the thinly covered boards and pulled a blanket round me, but fresh air and the unfamiliar plip, plop of water dripping from wet leaves soon lulled me into peaceful sleep.

Nothing was more perfect than waking early next morning, and peeping under the awning I saw a faint hint of sunshine filtering through the patterned leaves. I listened to the gentle slap, slap of tiny wavelets splashing the side of the boat, and breathed the distinctive tang of weedy water.

An unmistakable smell of methylated spirit and sounds of popping and spluttering, abruptly ended my dreaming. I dressed hurriedly, climbed out of the punt into the crisp morning and scrambled up the bank. Already Father was crouched over the primus stove, with hands extended to protect its reluctant flame.

'It's nearly going,' he said, optimistically.

But we all knew the primus had problems. Either the wind was in the wrong direction and we had to help shield the tiniest flicker, or else the burner needed to be repeatedly 'pricked' to clear a blockage. Eventually, after much hissing, smoking and popping, the flame settled down and the small camping kettle began to boil. I helped flatten the ground sheet over the bumpy grass, then collected plates and cutlery from our punt. And on that first morning — like every morning on our holiday — came the mouth-watering sound and smell of sizzling bacon.

With breakfast over, the two awnings had to be rolled up and tied along the central strut of each punt, and the bedding neatly stowed behind the seats before being covered with a ground sheet.

'Let's go!' called the boys, impatiently, from the other boat. And we set off up the winding river.

As we neared Marsh Lock, the big grey gates slowly opened and we nosed our way in, carefully steering to one side.

'Grab that chain, someone. . .'

'Hold it loosely through your fingers, or we'll tip up!'

We bumped against the lock's slimy green sides, and someone from each boat grabbed a dangling chain to steady us in the eddying water as the level rose. Soon I found myself looking over the steep sides at small, neat flower beds. Once the level had steadied, we filled containers with fresh water, paid 6d for each punt to go through the lock, and made use of the public lavatories.

Leaving Marsh Lock we paddled on to Shiplake, followed by a family of swans. We passed a little house called *Rivercot*, where seventeen years earlier David had been born. Then we headed on upstream towards Sonning, Mapledurham, Pangbourne and Goring. Everyone took turns to sit at the stern and paddle alternately, first one side and then the other, to steer a straight course. If we wanted to go faster, to catch a lock before it closed for the night, two paddlers sat side by side, dipping rhythmically into the water.

I liked it when we could help open the sluices on the lock gates, by turning the heavy wheels. On smaller unmanned locks, or when the lock keeper was busy, we opened the gates too. We pressed our backs against the long extended bar, until each giant gate slowly swung open, letting the swirling water flow through. In the background rose the roar of the weir, and I watched the white cascade tumbling to a lower level.

At one lock we approached, we saw several people standing on the side staring into the water. 'Can't go through yet,' someone called.

'What's happened?'

'There's an iron rod jammed in one of the gates. They're sending a diver from Thames Conservancy to shift it.'

So we steered to one side and held on to a chain, gently rocking in the lock as precious time slipped by. Eventually, a diver equipped with helmet, pipe lines, macintosh waders and huge brass boots climbed awkwardly down a long ladder into the water. We watched air bubbles coming to the surface as he moved about, and soon the obstruction was cleared. The excitement over, we paid our sixpences to the lock keeper and glided between the heavy wooden gates.

Sometimes we bought home-grown produce from a lock-keeper's wife, or when we came to a village we tied the punts to a convenient tree, and with ration books in hand went to buy food and explore the unknown places. Then back we would go with our provisions to set off once more, paddling our way upstream.

'Raining again,' one of us would shout, and we hastily made for the nearest bank.

'Quick, help me get the awning down. Everything's getting soaked.' But almost as suddenly, the sun would shine and we continued our leisurely way up the green dimpled river.

My mind was mulling over a plot for *The Mystery of the Ruined Boathouse*, which Mother had suggested as the title of a story, to be written when we returned home. To give scope to my imagination, I conjured up the carefree settings of Arthur Ransome's *Swallows and Amazons*, for by now I was immersed in the adventures of John, Susan, Titty and Roger,

I collected boat names in a homemade alphabetical book, too. 'Look at that smashing boat!' I said, when I spotted the occasional magnificent launch moored to a private landing stage, and I scribbled down the name in my book.

Steamers chugged by, bearing the names of riverside towns and villages, and we waved to the passengers. But when a steamer or

Steamers chugged by

motor boat came too close, our punts rocked and splashed alarmingly in their threatening bow waves. Along the bank we watched river birds, and caught a glimpse of shy water voles darting into their holes. Sometimes we played French cricket or rounders, and when the bank sloped gently we bathed in the clear water.

Gliding under overhanging branches, watching the sun sinking through a pink-speckled sky, sleeping surrounded by softly lapping water, time, like the river, slowly drifted by. All too soon we were back once more within sight of Henley; our holiday nearly over. We collected my bicycle from the repair shop, and started on the homeward journey to Dulwich.

Almost as soon as we returned from holiday, the new term started. I always had a strange uncertain feeling, after the long summer break, waiting by the top netball court for the cloakroom doors to open. There was a familiarity about it all, yet a newness too. The girls were the same, yet somehow they looked different. The building was the same, but I saw it with different eyes. The school was the same, although I had a different classroom. Who would I sit next to? Could I sit by the window? What would the form mistress be like? But I soon settled in as another autumn term unfolded.

As Christmas approached, Nigel and I cycled to Brixton as usual, to wander round buying our presents. But Christmas had ceased to be that shining beacon, guiding the year. The bubble had burst and sadly some of the magic had disappeared. Even so, there was still the same feeling of involvement, and buying our presents was just as important.

'Look at that,' whispered Nigel, as we mingled with shoppers in Woolworth's.

I looked to where he was indicating and saw a small man furtively looking around. His hand slid over a pair of striped braces, and in an instant he had gathered them up and slipped them under his shabby brown coat.

'Let's follow him,' I whispered back.

The man sidled past another counter, glanced sideways to see if an assistant was watching, then swiftly snatched at an item and moved on. Unobtrusively we eyed his crafty pilfering, but no one else seemed to notice.

'He's heading for the door now,' said Nigel. 'Come on we'll tail him.'

Keeping a safe distance we followed the man past the shops, weaving in and out of shoppers to keep him in sight. He didn't look back but kept on walking. A short way along the road he disappeared into the unkempt garden of a run-down house. Nigel signalled to me to keep out of sight, then pulling up the collar of his long fawn raincoat, he strode confidently after the shoplifter.

In recent months Nigel had grown taller and 'leggy', and by raising himself up he seemed taller still. He lowered his voice to a gruff pitch and called after the man, 'Hey, you, I'm from the police!'

The man stopped suddenly and turned round as Nigel, with collar up shielding his face, said he had been watching the shoplifting. The man looked at the ground, shuffling his feet until Nigel added, 'I'll let you off this time!' and ruined the allusion.

When we reached home, we told David all about it. But we knew we would soon be unable to rush back and tell David our news, for life was about to change.

12. Almost Grown-Up: 1949-1952

'What do you think David has for breakfast?'
'Where do you think he'll be posted?'
'I wonder what time he gets up?'
We clamoured for details when David went off to Oudenarde Barracks in Aldershot, to start his eighteen months' compulsory National Service. After his initial training and inoculations, early in 1949, his letters mentioned the possibility of being posted to Singapore or Kenya, and I thought of all the foreign stamps I might get. So we were surprised when he eventually went to Maryhill Barracks in Glasgow, where he learnt to type and do shorthand.

To relieve the boredom of routine he sent home detailed letters, and we soon found his new way of life had become an extension of our own. We were fascinated to receive his news, as if he were an explorer penetrating uncharted lands. However mundane, we mulled over and discussed every nugget of information.

'I got paid 31s this week and have already spent 8s 7d on my shoes and 10d on stamps,' we learned from one letter. 'But I sold my cigarette coupons for 2s.' In another letter he wrote, 'This weekend I hope to repeat last week's procedure and have my weekly hot bath for 10d!'

If we saw the postman coming up the path, one of us hurried to the door to see if there was a letter from David. Then chivvied by Mother we wrote back as often as we could.

'I'm going to tell David about my new macintosh we bought for 15s instead of 42s,' I said. 'And my new beret for 6s 11d.' I also told him about Mother's new hat — a tiny 'pill box', with a fine feather that stood up, quivering with the slightest movement. But Nigel's news was far more interesting.

'They're pulling down the underground shelters in the Townley Road field,' he reported, when he returned from school one day. 'It's going to be a war memorial garden. And they've pulled up the concrete slabs where the barrage balloon used to be.' He sent the details to David, with news of football, cross-country running and other school activities.

Later, when Nigel came back from a field day on Epsom Downs with the school cadets, he wrote about the day's activities: 'We had smoke bombs, sten guns, bren guns, rifles and rubber knives. But Sergeant King shot me in the back and our bren gun post was captured, so that was the end of it for me!'

Sadly news of Fluff being 'put to sleep' because of pleurisy and pneumonia also had to be related to David, together with the day-to-day events Mother regularly sent him: 'Nigel and his friend Roy have gone to Brixton Astoria to see *Private Angels*. Nigel received his pay today for school harvest camp — £2 8s 6d — so they are celebrating.'

I heard the telephone ring when I was in the playroom and I heard Mother talking. Then the receiver clicked and she came to find me. 'That was Sheila Moon's mother,' she said. 'To see if we would allow you to go on holiday with them to Swalecliffe.'

'*Allow* me to go, of *course* I can go!' I said, optimistically.

Going away without the family; what a wonderful idea! It added to my feeling of independence, for I was gradually emerging into the grown-up world. My waist-length hair had been cut off and my hair styled, mainly — so I was told — to stop all my energy from 'going to my hair'. Even so, it was a mark of growing maturity.

I began, straight away, preparing for the promised holiday. I would need new dresses, decent underwear and pyjamas. Sheila was always neatly dressed, so there could be none of my old frocks and skirts I wore in the woods. Although clothing coupons were no longer needed, money was permanently short, so I carefully cut out and machined two passable dresses from material Auntie Gladys had given me, which I had been reluctant to use.

'Can I take your copy of *War and Peace?*' I said, reading the titles along the bookshelves in the dining room. 'I need a large book to last two weeks.' Mother seemed dubious, but I packed the book in my case, which was slowly filling up.

When the longed-for day arrived, Mr Moon's big black Austin drew up by the kerb. Father helped load my case into the boot, while the two mothers chatted. Then stepping on to the running board, I climbed in the back with Sheila and sank into the luxury of soft leather.

'Good-bye, have a lovely holiday,' my parents called.

'I'll send some post cards. Will you keep them for my collection?'

We all waved as the car moved off, out along the vaguely familiar route towards Kent, which I had cycled on our memorable journey to Whitstable. Sheila and I giggled our way to the sea under her mother's attentive eye, while her father drove with just the occasional grunt or comment. I liked Sheila's parents. Without spoiling or lacking in firmness, Mrs Moon, tall, slim and elegant, seemed to control us with an almost humorous understanding. I felt at ease when I was with her, with no need to be on my best behaviour. Even so, I knew when this was called for.

As Sheila and I unpacked, I saw the titles *True Murders* and *True Romances* in amongst her clothes. Sheila had been more realistic about her holiday reading, so we both avidly read the lurid magazines and hid them away when we left our room.

One dark night I woke suddenly and found Sheila sitting bolt upright in the double bed we shared. 'If she comes she'll kill!' she said in a menacing voice. Then still sleeping she lay down again.

Next morning, when we were talking and laughing about her outburst, Mrs Moon suddenly came into the bedroom. 'I think I'd better look at those magazines you're always reading,' she said.

Horrified by the contents she vetted all the stories, and to our amazement put us on our honour not to read one of them.

'I don't see why I can't read it,' I said to Sheila, when her mother had left the room. 'Then I can tell you what it's about.'

'No!' said Sheila, adamantly. 'My mother's in charge of you while you're on holiday, so you've got to. . .'

'Yes, but. . .' I tried to interrupt.

'Her rules apply to us both,' Sheila said, firmly.

In the end neither of us read the story — and neither were the covers of *War and Peace* opened.

I enjoyed my holiday in Swalecliffe, staying with Mrs Moon's elderly aunts, Lally and Gertrude, and I wrote post cards home, telling of the country walks to Chestfield to see the oast house by a tiny pond, and the church in the wood. I wrote about fishing with hand lines from Herne Bay pier; miniature golf; the visits to Dreamland, the reptile house and the monkey zoo at Margate; the 'lights' at Ramsgate — all the traditional holiday activities I hadn't known before.

Sheila and I also dug for cockles on the wide flat sand and

boiled them up in the kitchen for a 'snack'. And on one memorable evening we dressed neatly and went to a country hotel for a *real* evening meal. I was unused to eating out — except at the Grafton Hall for 'British Restaurant' meals — so I sat timidly watching to see how to eat the cantaloupe melon placed in front of me.

'Would you like some ginger, Margaret?' asked Mrs Moon. But I was afraid to sprinkle ginger over the melon, as the other's were doing, in case it made me cough.

Mr Moon, with much patience, tried to teach me to swim, but it was Sheila who finally succeeded in getting me to do a few strokes. And once I had learnt, I practised swimming between the breakwaters until I became proficient. That holiday, and on all my holidays at Swalecliffe with the Moons, Sheila and I sang the latest songs as we walked along the beach. We talked about boys, giggled, joked and questioned each other in our usual way. And we grew up just a little more.

Soon after I returned home, I wrote to David telling him all about it. Nigel and I mostly scribbled our letters in the playroom between bouts of homework. Our parents wrote letters in the playroom, too, and sometimes, surrounded by pieces of cut wool, they made rugs or Mother made lampshades. Occasionally we managed to fit in a restricted game of table-tennis on the playroom table, or a card game of Rummy, Queens or Whist. And we always found time for the inevitable 'paper games'.

'I bet I remember *everything*,' Nigel boasted, 'next time we play Twenty Things.'

Chestfield Oasthouse

'I bet you don't!' I said.

But when twenty small objects were placed on a tray for us to memorise and write down, Nigel knew them all.

'It's simple. One bun, two shoe, three tree,' he said, annoyingly. 'I've got a list to remember them by.'

'How?'

'Just picture each thing on the tray with a word on the list.' And he taught me his list.

'One bun, two shoe, three tree, four door, five knife . . .' I said over and over, until I knew them all up to twenty. And next time we played 'Twenty Things' I completed the list too.

That autumn Uncle Keith taught Nigel how to play chess, so Nigel taught me the rules and I set up a league which included our parents, and David when he was home on leave. I was aware that our joint activities were all part of Mother's 'sense of family', as she called it, and that listening to concerts, 'Saturday Night Theatre' and variety shows on the radio, and my favourite 'Much Binding in the Marsh', were just as important.

'You know why, don't you?' said Nigel, when we were alone.

'Why what?'

'Why she wants a *sense of family*.' And he proceeded to tell me that when Mother was eight and Auntie Gladys six, their own mother had left home. The two little girls were looked after by friends or housekeepers until Grandpa finished his army career, and Mother, at fourteen, managed the house.

Now I understood why the family meant so much to her, and how our letter-writing would keep David involved.

At 5.30 on a mild January morning, Father's alarm clock shrilled out. Almost immediately he was out of bed, sitting on the side pulling on his socks as he always did — though not usually so early. At 5.45 I was up too, and by 6.30 we had walked through Dulwich Village to the dimly-lit station at North Dulwich, where we caught a train to London Bridge.

I settled myself in the corner, listening to the rhythmic sounds overlaid one with another, as I tried to glimpse the passing houses through the dark mirrored windows. I was glad we had started so early, it meant we would have a whole day on the south coast, where Father had some business appointments. But for me it was going to be a wonderful day's outing.

From London Bridge we caught a train to Seaford, changing at Lewes where we had a cup of tea in the station restaurant. Soon afterwards, in the connecting train, we ate home-made cheese sandwiches, for we seldom went anywhere without copious supplies of Father's sandwiches.

At Seaford Father went off to visit two shops, while I stood in a sheltered patch of warming sunshine watching tumbling water breaking over the sea wall. Spray leapt high in the air, with a fresh, tangy smell of winter sea. A little later, travelling over the South Downs by bus to Newhaven, we ate more 'special' sandwiches — this time they were egg.

We moved on along the coast to Rottingdean, where I explored the quaint old streets, passing ancient houses and a pond to discover St Margaret's church. From here we caught a bus to Brighton and I noticed a sign to Ovingdean, where Auntie Polly and Aunt Editha once lived. The bus turned towards the sea and we travelled on along the coast road, watching waves crashing over the rocky headland.

'There's a little brown train down there,' I said, as the bus moved on. 'It's running along a narrow track at the edge of the beach. It's only about a quarter the size of a real carriage.'

'Can you see there's a wheel at each end?' Father pointed them out, before the bus rattled on and I looked out across the ragged waves once more. When we reached Brighton we saw the beach-train again, coming in to its tiny station, and within minutes another was setting off.

Brighton seemed to be full of cinemas, Woolworth's and Lyons cafés to me. At one Lyons, we stopped for fish and chips and a cup of tea before setting off again, walking along the shop-lined streets. By 4.30 we were down by the sea, sliding across slippery pebbles for a last look at the waves before our journey home.

During the day Father had mentioned the *Brighton Belle*, but I just thought it was one of the made-up names he was apt to use. But when we reached the station, I saw an unfamiliar train with brown and cream carriages waiting by the platform. I had expected it to be the usual Southern Railway green.

'It's a Pullman isn't it, like the Golden Arrow?' I peered through the windows in delight. 'It's just like a hotel on wheels!'

We chose a carriage and climbed in, and to my surprise I found that each section of four seats had a table with a lamp, curtains at the windows and a bell above our heads. As we selected our seats, a voice came over the loud speaker: 'Ladies and gentlemen, it is now 5.20 and the Brighton Belle will be leaving at 5.25. Will all visitors who are not travelling please leave the train. Thank you.'

Promptly at 5.25 the magnificent train pulled out of Brighton Station and we settled down to enjoy the journey back to London.

'Look, there're waiters in white tail-coats walking up and down the gangway, ' I whispered to Father.

'Serving buttered toast, cake and tea,' he said, as a tray was being unloaded on to our table.

At Victoria, another announcement hoped we had a comfortable journey. 'Which indeed we have!' I said, then added, 'I've got *real* news to tell David now.'

One morning, when I looked to see if there was a letter from David, I saw one with a Canadian stamp.

'It's from Jim Wheatley.' Father sounded surprised when I gave him the letter, although I knew he seldom heard from his Canadian second cousin.

'Jim's coming to England with Marge and the children, and wonders if we can put them up for three weeks.' I heard him say to Mother.

'Would we have room for them all? How old are the children?'

'Let's see . . .Jo's six and Bruce is three.'

'They could have David's room, if they don't mind the squash.'

Soon details of the visit were arranged, and I was there with Nigel and our parents to welcome them when they arrived. During the day they all went sight-seeing, and each evening recounted stories of places they had visited and sights they had seen. They spoke of seeing preparations for the Festival of Britain, which was soon due to open, and the bomb damage in our 'quaint, old-fashioned London' constantly amazed them.

Jo somehow became my responsibility, particularly after supper when she went to bed. I would read story after story to her, then tuck her up for the night, but she would be out of bed again before I had left the room. One evening when I was trying to get her into her pyjamas, with arms and legs flying in all directions, Jo 'escaped' and rushed downstairs. I chased after her and found her parading naked in front of the grown-ups in the dining room. Full of embarrassment I collected my charge. No one should be seen *naked* I thought, not even a six-year-old!

But I enjoyed their rushed visit, with stories of Canada and a glimpse of a wider world, so the three weeks sped by. On their final day, Marge gave Mother and me a small package each, which we opened before they left.

'*Nylon stockings!* Thank you!' I said with delight. 'We can't buy nylons over here.' I carefully placed my pair in my dressing table drawer, saving them for special occasions — and rarely wore them.

Soon after their visit, David's National Service ended, so he left the regular army and became a Territorial for a further three-and-a-half years. At weekends he went off in his uniform again, but I was glad he wouldn't be involved with the Korean war which had just broken out.

Uncle John, David's godfather and a director of a London tie manufacturer, offered David a job. So with no other immediate prospects, David travelled by train each morning from North Dulwich to London Bridge, and then on to Frank Theak and Roskilly in the City. One evening I heard him telling Mother about someone at 'Theaks', who lived in Manchester and was looking for a place to stay during the week.

'He could stay here if he doesn't mind the boxroom,' suggested Mother. 'Why don't you invite him back for a meal so we can meet him?'

I couldn't wait to see Gwilym Hefin Evans, it was such a lovely name! When he arrived I immediately liked the soft lilt of his partly Welsh and partly Mancunian accent, so I was glad when Gwilym settled in with us. But young men of David's age were still beyond my reach, although this didn't stop me from admiring Gwilym from afar. Each morning I stood at my bedroom window, watching him going off to work in his neat grey suit, with a trilby hat tilted to an almost rakish angle. And on one exciting evening he helped me with my German homework.

Stacking the washed dishes on the wooden draining board in the scullery the next day, I sang at the top of my voice: 'You are my heart's delight and where you are I long to be.' Thinking I was alone I rose to a full crescendo with 'Shine and my whole life through. . .' when the side door opened and in came Gwilym, grinning. Red with embarrassment I fled from the room.

We were studying a new subject at school now, called Current

Affairs and Citizenship, where I heard how Marshal Aid from America was gradually helping Britain and Europe in the slow recovery from the war. We learnt about the difficulty of organisation and how essential supplies had run down. Industry had to be rebuilt and many bomb-sites still needed to be cleared. As a stop-gap prefabs had been erected, but now permanent houses were needed.

The formation of the United Nations; the North Atlantic Treaty Organisation; rapidly deteriorating relations with Russia; Communist governments installed in Poland, Rumania, Bulgaria, Hungary and Czechoslovakia were all discussed in detail, so too was Russia's closing of the routes to the Western Sector of Berlin, causing supplies to be airlifted in. But to me it was still part of the wider world, and home and school were far more important.

I had worked well in the first three years of the senior school, and one Saturday, as form hockey captain, I took my team to Brockwell Park to practice, until a park keeper came hurrying over. 'You can't play here,' he had said. 'You're a danger to the public!'

In the upper fourth, with great pride, I came top in biology and fourth in history. But in September, when we moved up to the lower fifth, things changed. We saw at once that our new form mistress was not just new to the school, but new to teaching girls in their teens. Her problem, we realised, was lack of discipline; our downfall was knowing it.

Our new form mistress also took us for religious knowledge and history, and once we found out that her father was a vicar, and that she had a considerable knowledge of the Bible, we angled all conversations around religion so we could argue. Audaciously we disputed every point she made, and at home I studied the Bible to get more 'ammunition' to counter her discrepancies. The new teacher, fearing the increasing chaos in her class, was almost relieved to be involved in a religious discussion. The fact that it should have been a history lesson didn't seem to matter.

Knowing we were 'getting away with it', we realised we could get away with other things too. After one of our innumerable sales for the school swimming bath fund, a large lump of soft, greasy toffee was left over. It had been dropped on the ground, picking up grit and dirt when it rolled under a table. Someone took the toffee back to the classroom and threw it across to a friend, sitting by the window. The toffee hit the glass and slid slowly down the pane, as we tried to stifle our wild laughter.

'Catch it!'

'Throw it back!'

The words hissed across the classroom, and before the new teacher could see it, the toffee was grabbed and hurled back. This time it hit the glass-panelled inner wall with another satisfying thud, accompanied by more, almost hysterical, laughter.

There was no stopping us after that. The toffee whizzed backwards and forwards across the room. Splat! it went on the window. Slap, it hit the inner wall. It was never seen or confiscated by the new teacher; there were too many other distractions for her to notice. Irritatingly the toffee sometimes landed on our open books, leaving a dirty mark, or it hit one of us, leaving a greasy stickiness over hair and clothes.

'If we all knock a pile of books off our desks at the same time,' someone suggested, tiring of toffee throwing, 'it'll make a smashing noise!'

At precisely 3 o'clock the books landed on the floorboards and the resounding clatter successfully stopped all work.

'Pick up your books, girls,' was the quiet response from the new teacher, so we looked for other distractions.

One day, unbeknown to David, I borrowed his Brownie box camera. With girls wandering round the class and others leaning over the teacher's desk, I aimed the camera ready for a suitably disorganised picture. I took two, and surprisingly the camera wasn't seen — or if it had been nothing was said. We were on a high with success, so our once well-behaved, hard-working class rapidly deteriorated in other lessons, too, although other teachers were more vigilant.

On a rare visit to Kew Gardens, the new teacher thought we were being particularly polite. We opened the door of a hot-house to see the plants, and one by one stood back to let her go in first. Smiling at our courtesy she stepped inside, then hurriedly the door was closed behind her and we raced off to explore on our own. Delighted by our successes, we didn't realise the damage that was being done, until our end-of-term reports went home.

'Margaret is capable of a better standard of work and behaviour.' Father read out Miss Gordon Ewen's comment, as I stood in the dining room with my parents, and tried to think of a suitable excuse.

'What does this mean, Margaret? Aren't you *working* at school?' Mother was shocked. 'And not *behaving?*'

They were even more astonished at a parents' evening, when the new teacher said I was the ringleader of all the trouble in the class. I knew I wasn't — we were all involved. But how could I tell my parents what was happening?

It wasn't just my class. We laughed with delight when we heard about one form, lower down the school. They had tied strong black cotton across the gangways between the desks, and for a time successfully prevented the new teacher from walking down them. But soon, although our religious arguments continued, an unexpected buzz was going round the lower fifth, so we had other things to think about.

'Have you heard?' someone said. 'We're going to have dancing lessons after school next term.'

'Where?' 'When?' We clamoured for details.

'On Fridays in the hall.'

At the end of the Easter holidays, in readiness for the forthcoming dances, I tried on my best dress.

'It's too tight,' Mother said in dismay, trying to close the back fasteners. 'You must have grown.'

'It was getting tight for Sheila's outing,' I reminded her. 'Can I have a new one?'

'I'm afraid not. Not before Friday anyway.'

I knew money was a permanent problem, but I couldn't possibly go to the dance in my brown check *school* dress.

'I wonder if I've got one you could wear,' Mother said, hopefully.

So we searched through her wardrobe, selecting and discarding familiar dresses until I found one I thought suitable to try on. I looked in the mirror at my burgeoning figure, concealed under Mother's dress, while she waited, tentatively.

'It's perfect!' I said, at last. 'My first grown-up frock!' And I went off happily to hang it in my own wardrobe.

The following Friday, I clattered down the concrete stairs to the cloakroom with Mary Marsh and our friends, to change out of our uniforms. Then, giggling and chattering, we walked more sedately up the stairs again to the hall. But we were confronted with bitter disappointment.

'It's not fair. We've got to dance with each other. They might have asked a *boys'* school!'

'You can be the man,' I said to Mary. 'You're taller than me.' In this way I knew I would learn the female steps. But despite our initial disappointment, we all agreed that our first school dance was a great success.

With a wonderful sense of anticipation everyone had been looking forward to the 1951 Festival of Britain, which was to last from May until September. As we wandered round the exhibits, housed in pavilions around the new Festival Hall, I was overawed by the mass of arts and crafts and the almost unbelievable scientific achievements. I looked up at the slender, futuristic 'Skylon', rising above the vast roof of the Dome of Discovery, where I marvelled at the latest inventions and exploits of famous explorers. Equally exciting were the Festival Pleasure Gardens at Battersea Park, with a fun-fair, open-air theatre and model railway; all beautifully floodlit by night.

Suddenly, Britain had come alive again after years of drabness. I vaguely remembered the 'Britain Can Make It' exhibition back in 1946, but that had been a fraction of the size. Enthusiasm for the Festival spread throughout the country. Our letters had special festival postage stamps which I collected. We saw colourful commemorative goods in the shops, and we heard that many trees were being planted and seats donated in memory of the event.

At St Martin's we worked hard for our own ambitious gymnastics display, when the school field was marked out with intersecting white lines for the disciplined, rhythmic displays. With a feeling of pride, dressed in a specially-made short white tunic I, and 499 other girls, marched on to the field. We took up our well-rehearsed positions, then swung and gyrated our way through the timed movements.

We put on a dancing display, too, when each year represented a different country in costume and dance. Mary Marsh and I danced in time with our fellow 'Norwegian' couples, and after long weeks of practice, we felt our school's contribution to the festivities had been an impressive sight.

The hectic summer term was almost over when another buzz went round the lower fifth, and we excitedly discussed it among ourselves. 'Are you going to Battersea Grammar next term?'

'Battersea Grammar? What for?'

'They have dances every week in the autumn term.'

'Who's going?'

Disciplined, rhythmic gymnastics

School group by the tennis court

Anne	Margaret	Barbara
Hamilton	Simmonds	Bowthorpe
author	Annette	Sheila
front left	Darlington	Moon

The dancing display

Sheila and I wanted to go along, but we realised this meant we would have to wait for one of the Battersea boys to ask us to dance. That, we thought, would be far too embarrassing. Supposing no one asked us? We talked over the problem and agreed it would be better to persuade Nigel and his friend Roy, from Alleyn's, to come with us.

'We'll show you the steps first,' we told them. 'Then you'll know what to do.' So in the summer holidays we manoeuvred them awkwardly through the basic steps of the waltz, quickstep, foxtrot and tango.

'Forward side together; forward side together,' we repeated, pulling them round the playroom. And, 'Slow, slow, quick, quick, slow.' It was then that we remembered the black portable gramophone Auntie Gladys had recently given David.

'Can we borrow it? How does it work?' I asked him.

'You wind it up with this handle,' David explained, 'open out this chrome arm and lower it on to the record.'

'Can we borrow it then?'

'Yes, but if a record sounds scratchy you *must* change the needle. Take the old one out and slot in a new one.' And he gave me a supply of fine-pointed metal needles.

Now, as Nigel and Sheila, and Roy and I danced round the playroom, we became entangled in the tango with Sheila's record of 'La Compasita'. And when Victor Sylvester's version of 'June is Busting Out All Over' resounded through the house, we perfected our quickstep.

On an earlier trip to Oxford Street with Mother, I had taken time selecting and buying the Victor Sylvester record from Selfridges' music department. It was the first record I had bought, so I chose with care, listening to several in a small record booth before making up my mind. In the holidays, too, we went to Brixton to buy my first pair of court shoes and my long-awaited dress. And now I would be able to wear my precious nylon stockings.

When the Festival of Britain ended that September, there seemed to be a slight down-turn in feelings once the excitement had gone. Even so, the Festival Hall and Pleasure Gardens remained.

'At least it shows the country's getting back on its feet again,' said Mother. 'And rationing *surely* can't go on much longer?'

I knew many items had already been de-rationed, including

clothes, soap, bread and some foods. But bacon, cheese, fats and meat still needed coupons. Sweets, having been taken off ration, had gone back on again because of the rush to buy them.

It was not a surprise, when we started back at school for the autumn term, to find that the new teacher had left St Martin's. And we didn't really think about the damage that had been done, while we had fooled around in the first vital year of out two-year O-level course. We had other things to think about.

Soon, dancing round the Battersea Grammar School hall, to the strains of Victor Sylvester on gramophone records, became the highlight of each week. We mixed more freely with boys now, instead of being in our enclosed, all-girl community, and we chattered and giggled through the evenings. Occasionally we noticed a dancing pair had disappeared to darker recesses of the school, and we waited eagerly for the daring girl to report back on her experiences of petting and 'French kissing'.

As the term progressed, we also found ourselves caught up in the third general election since the war. Back in July 1945, when 'my war' ended, Labour had won a landslide victory under Clement Attlee, the Deputy Prime Minister in the wartime coalition government. We had noticed great changes taking place when the Welfare State was introduced, with free National Health Service, free school milk, pensions and unemployment money for all. And when vital industries had been nationalised, we talked at school about 'our' trains and 'our' coal mines.

At the same time Britain was critically short of money. Post-war years seemed as frugal as war years, and people blamed the government. So in the 1950 election we had not been surprised when Labour's majority was cut to seven.

Now, in October 1951, another election was necessary. Posters were displayed, leaflets distributed and at school we held a mock election. At home, we eagerly scanned the newspapers, greeting each piece of election news with appropriate glee or gloom.

On the actual night, when the results were coming in, we had 'beds' on the floor near the radio, snoozing until the music faded for a result to be announced. Then we were wide awake with pencils ready to mark each one on our printed newspaper charts, booing or cheering as they came through. Once again Father made his special sandwiches, and we had cups of tea at intervals until the radio eventually closed down in the early hours of the morning.

This time, when the final results came through, the Conservatives were elected, with Winston Churchill back in Downing Street.

As the eventful term came to an end, we heard there would be an eliminating dancing competition at Battersea Grammar School. On the final evening, we danced hopefully through the programme, as gradually couples were eliminated. To our surprise Roy and I came third — but I was even more surprised when I won the ankle competition. Secretly I thanked Marge for my nylon stockings.

I didn't really appreciate that Father's deep-felt religious principles had led him to resign from his job on more than one occasion. But I did know that he loved selling, and even though he was a member of the Incorporated Sales Managers' Association, he spent as much time selling as managing. So provided he had a job, and home life seemed stable, I was happy.

To help with ever-increasing bills, he started teaching English to commercial students at evening colleges in nearby Forrest Hill, Catford and Lewisham. But he loved teaching as much as selling.

We had all relaxed when he became business manager of a craft firm in London's Baker Street, where he edited *The Craft Journal* and organised a national craft exhibition. Mother wrote a 'Home Page' of useful craft ideas, and David contributed some of the drawings for the magazine. And on one occasion David had given me 6d for posing my hand on the playroom table, as a model for the 'working fingers' he was trying to draw.

It was soon after this that I heard discussions going on about Uncle Basil and Robert setting up their own craft factory. But I didn't take much notice until Father brought home strips of 'wool-twist' the factory produced.

'It looks like very fat pipe cleaners,' I said.

'That's how it's made, only these pieces can be bent and shaped into little furry animals,' Father explained.

I looked at the pieces, bending and twisting them into different shapes, while my parents continued talking about Uncle Basil's latest project.

'Outworkers to make the animals?' queried Mother.

'Yes, and I'll sell them.'

'But is it really *secure?*'

Once the factory was well established, near Uncle Basil's home in Wallington, Father left *The Craft Journal* to set up as a manufacturers' agent, to market the furry animals and other toys throughout the country. Mother was persuaded to become an outworker, bending, teazling and clipping the wool-twist into tiny cats, bears and rabbits.

Soon, I was bending, teazling and clipping, too. With strong-smelling glue, always ready for use heating in a saucepan of water on the gas stove, we attached the eyes and whiskers. I was pleased to have spare money, but although the outwork gradually increased we had deadlines to keep and the pay was not generous.

'I've had an idea, Margar,' said Mother, as we sat at the playroom table, trying to complete our latest quota of toys. 'Why don't we start our own business?'

'Our own business?' I said, and listened to her idea of buying strips of wool-twist from Uncle Basil, to make into similar animals which we would then dress.

'Mrs Mop can wear a little check apron with matching duster in one paw and a mop in the other. And we could make Puss-in-Boots. . .'

David designed and made the miniature red felt boots, complete with cardboard soles, for Puss-in-Boots, who carried over his shoulder a tiny check bundle on a thin plastic rod. We also made other animals and dressed them in matching or toned felt collars, belts and buttons. It was much more fun than mass-producing animals as an outworker. We were thrilled when orders for our dressed animals came in from Liberty's, Hamley's and Selfridges, as well as Father's other customers.

Through the foggy winter repeat orders piled up, but sadly we realised many of them could not be fulfilled. Nobody knew whether the fine dust created by teazling the wool had aggravated a chest infection, or whether it was the result of the enveloping, sulphurous London smog. But Mother developed bronchitis, which rapidly turned to bronchial pneumonia.

With no central heating, an electric fire was kept permanently on in her bedroom to maintain a minimum temperature of 65°F. It seemed stiflingly hot to me, when I went in to see her. And the room was filled with a curious medicinal smell, too; a mixture of kaolin poultice and friars balsam 'steam bath'. To keep the steam permanently ready, Father had placed the bowl of friars balsam in a saucepan of water, which rested on the metal safety bars of the electric fire. This, in turn, lay on its back on the floor. There was no thought of the extreme danger of this arrangement. It was simply the most practical. Periodically the bowl was placed on a tray, and Mother, with head under a towel, inhaled the steam.

Preparing the kaolin poultice was a sticky, tricky business, so early each morning Auntie Madge — a trained Red Cross nurse — arrived on her bicycle to administer the treatment. We heard painful laughter coming from the room, despite the severity of the illness, as Auntie Madge tried to strap the unwieldy poultice to Mother's chest.

'No, Madeline, it goes the other way,' croaked Mother.

'Keep still, Lilian dear.'

I was given permission to arrive late for school each morning, so that I could tidy up and prepare Mother for the day. I usually only missed the register and prayers, although sometimes I arrived in the middle of the first lesson. But now that I had a legitimate reason for being late, I no longer feared using the school's front entrance.

Slowly, Mother began to recover, and early in the new year, after much discussion, my parents decided we should move away from London into the country, before the following winter and more thick yellow smog. I didn't want to move and leave my friends behind, but I knew the smog had caused many deaths. Our own doctor, who lived on the opposite corner, sadly died from bronchial pneumonia while Mother was still recovering.

So once more, house details flopped through the letter box and we set off to see some of the properties. We searched and viewed over a wide area, until my parents set their heart on a small bungalow in a tiny hamlet called Harpsden, on the outskirts of Henley-on-Thames. The bungalow, set in yet another completely overgrown garden, had ancient gas mantles, no electricity and cesspit drainage. The contrast with our Dulwich house was enormous, but my parents fell in love with the picturesque wooded setting on the edge of Henley Golf Course, and knew there was potential for a beautiful garden.

Very soon the wheels of moving were in motion again, but this time, during weekdays, David, Nigel and I would be staying behind. The boys went to live in a flat not far from Dulwich, where David stayed until he left Theak and Roskilly to start his chosen career in journalism. Nigel's National Service was deferred, so he stayed in the flat to enable him to finish his A-levels. And I went to Wallington, with Uncle Basil, Auntie Ethel and Gill, and travelled each day by train to school.

The bungalow at Harpsden

'Mrs Moon has asked me to stay with them, to save me the train journey,' I had said, hoping I could stay with Sheila. But family connections always came first on these occasions.

I caught a brief glimpse of my future life in Harpsden, when every Friday evening I travelled from Paddington station to Henley for the weekend. During the journey I made a start on my homework or revised for my impending O-level exams. Then early on Monday morning I went back to Paddington and on to school. When Father was going in my direction he gave me a lift, and some weekends I stayed with Sheila or she travelled down to Henley with me. But it was a wonderful feeling, my unaccustomed independence.

Moving to Henley marked the end of my childhood. The war was already a distant memory, our involvement with Devizes, and our many home-made clubs, had long been outgrown. That summer, because of the distance I had to travel and the difficulties of getting to and from Henley, I sadly left St Martin's. Although this meant leaving my school friends behind, we had forged close links and continued to keep in touch.

But now, for me, a new adult life was waiting to begin.

Taïlpiece: 1995

No one would choose to grow up during a world war, but time has shown how much those austere years have taught me. Time has also shown that there are no civilians in war. Everyone is involved because survival depends on it. Even we children did our bit: saving salvage, raising money, economising with food, water, electricity; accepting life as it happened.

Today, like many who grew up in the forties, I still undo knots to save string; use the last slither of soap; re-use gift wrappings, envelopes and paper bags; write on the reverse side of printed paper; cut the empty toothpaste tube in half to reach the remaining contents. . . because adult actions are enmeshed with childhood roots.

But mingling with the frugality of my forties childhood, were the happy, imaginative times — 'Devizes', that wonderful world which cocooned us from a life of uncertainty, and became our antidote to war and postwar restrictions. Looking back, Devizes was also an excellent training ground for later life; a microcosm of adulthood, when we tested our reactions to the grown-up world before we became part of it. Devizes didn't die, it simply faded from prominence.

I still remember, as others remember, those warm summer scents of flowering privet and buddleia; heat rising from a dusty road; a sun that always seemed to be shining. And even after I emerged into my unknown future, I continued to cherish that wonderment of childhood, and I hope I have never lost it.

Acknowledgements

So that time could not distort the events of those war years, for part of my background research I used a series of six books which were published soon after the war, and are listed in the bibliography. The photographs, dates and details were then fresh in the minds of the photographers and writers. I also had access to many documents, letters, post cards and other family memorabilia, which helped bring those growing-up years into focus.

Visits to the Imperial War Museum and local studies libraries in South London, Swindon and Swansea were equally essential. And I read many first-hand accounts and diaries, written at the time of the events, so that I could absorb, once more, the feelings that were uppermost in our minds when the events took place.

My thanks go to my brothers, David and Nigel, for reading my draft manuscript, for their helpful comments and for jogging my memory.

Illustrations

I much appreciate permission to use the following illustrations: Morrison shelter from the Imperial War Museum; devastation of Swansea's town centre from Swansea City Archives; Milly-Molly-Mandy from the book by Joyce Lancaster Brisley, from Chambers Harrap; Gower Road Sketty from the Frith Collection; St Martin-in-the-Fields' High School drawn by David in his teens; and photographs from various members of the family.

Bibliography

Battles and Battlescenes of World War Two, David G. Chandler (Arms and Armour, 1989).

The Bleak Midwinter 1947, Alex J. Robertson (Manchester University Press, 1987).

British Intelligence in the Second World War (vol. 5 Strategic Deception), Michael Howard (HMSO, 1990).

The Doodlebugs: the story of the flying bombs, Norman Longmate (Hutchinson, 1981).

Hitler's Last Weapons, Jozef Garlinski (Julian Friedmann, 1978).

Hitler's Rockets: the story of the V2, Norman Longmate (Hutchinson, 1985).

Life in Wartime Britain (English Life series) edited by Peter Quennel and E.R. Chamberlain (Batsford, 1972).

The People's War, 1939-1945, Angus Calder (Jonathan Cape, 1986).

Radio: The Great Years, Derek Parker (David and Charles, 1977).

Struggle for Survival: R.A.C.Parker (Oxford University Press, 1989).

The War in Pictures — 6 volumes (Odhams).

The Way it Happened, 1935-1950, James MacMillan (William Kimber, 1980).